Enough for Today:

Encouragement to Trust In God

Sue Wunder

CROSSLINK
PUBLISHING

Enough for Today: Encouragement to Trust In God

CrossLink Publishing
www.crosslinkpublishing.com

ISBN 978-1-936746-97-2

Library of Congress Control Number: 2014930145

This book is dedicated to Mom and Dad, for so gracefully walking me through this life.

CONTENTS

Acknowledgments vii

Chapter 1 We Walk by Faith... 1

Chapter 2 The Hospital Chapel 7

Chapter 3 He Provides... 13

Chapter 4 The Gift of People 23

Chapter 5 Lessons Learned 29

Chapter 6 When God Sends Us 39

Chapter 7 Trusting God 45

Chapter 8 Where Was God? 55

Chapter 9 Listening and Praise.. 65

Chapter 10 An Expanded View 73

Chapter 11 How Can He Love Me? 89

Chapter 12 Salvaging After Loss.. 99

Chapter 13 Choosing To See Beauty....................................111

Chapter 14 An answer to My Prayer? 117

Chapter 15 What is Freedom? 125

ACKNOWLEDGMENTS

Rob, Robbie and Hailey - for supporting me in sharing our family journey. I know it is not always easy.

The rest of my amazing and ever-growing family – I love you guys!

My Caringbridge family – We shared a time. Many of those moments have become the pages of this book. I will be forever grateful.

My community of Cape May County – What an amazing rescue you made by coming together and supporting us emotionally, spiritually, and financially.

My school family at Cape May County Special Services - for your love and support. What an amazing group of people.

Debby - My closest friend in Christ. The day my faith met your knowledge, God began working on this book. Thanks for your involvement and your encouragement.

Patrick, Kyle, Tariq, and John – Robbie's fellow soldiers in the war of 2006 – I am always wishing each of you enough for each day.

The Langford family – for my home away from home.

Pastor Scott Durban – for your weekly encouragement.

CrossLink Publishing - for giving me the opportunity to share.

CHAPTER 1

We Walk by Faith

My eyes did not see God the night my sixteen-year-old son dove into a friend's swimming pool and broke his neck. My ears did not hear God telling me it would be all right. And I certainly did not feel His mighty arms lift me to my feet after I collapsed in the hospital corridor. But God was there, for as I walked by faith through that dark night, I knew I could only walk because of Him. It was not my eyes, nor my ears, nor the soft touch on my starving skin that comforted me. It was my faith in Him who has given me His word that He will never leave me. Yes, God was there, waiting for me to come running.

Hebrews 13:5 "Be content with what you have
because God has said 'Never will I leave you;
Never will I forsake you.'"

John 14:27 "Peace I leave with you. My peace I give you.
I do not give to you as the world gives.
Do not let your hearts be troubled
and do not be afraid."

It was just after 9:00 PM when my son and his girlfriend came home from a friend's house to get their bathing suits. "We're going for a swim down at Kayla's," my son said as his 6'2," 240-lb. frame filled the kitchen doorway, leaving little space for Amanda to peek in and say hello. They were so cute together. They had been dating for a little over a year, but for fifteen-year-old kids, they somehow had a really good idea about love.

It was not forty-five minutes later when two of Robbie's buddies were at my back door. "Come quick! Robbie's hurt, bad!" They were obviously panicked. My husband and I and our twelve-year-old daughter, Hailey, jumped into the car and raced down to the house where Robbie hung out at least a few days a week. There was already an ambulance, paramedics, a stability board, lights, sirens, confusion, then a helicopter. The next thing I knew, Robbie and I were being airlifted to the trauma unit at Jefferson Hospital in Philadelphia, Pa.

"Where's Amanda? I want Amanda with me! Please! Amanda!" The noise of the propellers drowned out his call as the heavy doors slammed shut on the world we once knew, and as we lifted up into the air, I could see Amanda standing alone in the dark, crying.

Robbie's breathing grew very shallow, and the paramedics were not sure he would make it to Philadelphia, so it was decided we would go to the Atlantic City trauma unit. When we arrived, a team of men and women clad in blue scrubs took their places around the gurney, gripped the metal rails, and raced off with my son. As I watched through the little square window in the now locked hallway door, I felt alone, helpless, and on such a warm summer night, I felt cold.

Robbie was an avid surfer. Whether there were waves or not, he was dedicated to the sport out of pure passion. I'm not sure if it was the rush of the ride or the peace that being out on the water brought him. I just know he loved it, and his perpetually peeling nose was evidence of time spent on the board. He also loved tearing up a dirt trail on his four-wheel, all-terrain vehicle. He got his first quad for Christmas when he was eleven years old. His second one, a much more powerful machine, he got a few years later and managed to make it even faster and louder than it already was. He would set out on a Saturday morning in his shiny helmet, chest guard, burnproof pants, boots, gloves, and goggles. And, every Saturday afternoon, he would return home unharmed and full of mud. Back then, mud was a sign that the day had been a good one.

Think about the gear with which we supplied our son before sending him out on his quad. We invested in every piece of equipment necessary to protect his body from harm—it was our responsibility as parents. I can honestly say we were not as diligent in attending to his spiritual safety. Perhaps we clad him more like Goliath than David. The 9-foot 9-inch Philistine wore a helmet, breastplate, shin guards all made of brass, and carried an iron spear in one hand and a shield in the other. But his physical stature and armor could not withstand the power of young David's faith in God. With only a staff and a sling, David killed Goliath with a single stone to the forehead. No matter how much we protect the body, without faith in what our God can do for us, we are vulnerable. Deep down, I wish we had invested more in our son's spiritual armor because now, with a paralyzed body, it will be what he carries inside that moves him.

Robbie's third passion was music. I had purchased an old guitar many years ago for five dollars at a yard sale and, one afternoon, Robbie decided to pick it up. He barely ever put it down again. He taught himself to play, and when we noticed the gift, we sent him for lessons. He amazed us at how quickly he learned new songs—and wasn't learning just cords, but picking and strumming like a professional. He was gifted. One of my favorite things in this lifetime will always be when I could sit in my kitchen and watch his fingers dance up and down the neck of his guitar. It was the sound of time spent together for him and me. It was the sound of an accomplishment. It was the sound of passion and promises of things to come. It was the sound of what I thought would be a part of Robbie's future. Well, it is now a sound that I have not heard since the night he dove into the pool.

"Mrs. Wunder?" The doctor finally came through the doors shortly after my husband Rob, Hailey, and Amanda arrived. "Would you please come with me?" He motioned for us all to follow. I thought we were going to see Robbie, but he led us into a conference room where we each took a place around a long wooden table surrounded by large, plush chairs. My husband took a seat by the doctor as Hailey and Amanda sat down at the same end of the table. Me, I sat as far away as possible, as if I didn't want the information to reach me. My hands were cold and my heart was hoping, but inside I already felt loss. "Your son has shattered his C5 vertebrae, leaving him paralyzed from the chest down." When the doctor explained to us that the only muscles my son would recover were his biceps, and explained how his fingers will never move again, the words crawled across the table like ugly little creatures with big black eyes, and came at me with their knifelike teeth and all intentions to kill me. I stood up and left the room.

CHAPTER 2

The Hospital Chapel

Suddenly, the sound of the helicopter door slamming shut echoed in my mind, and I panicked with the idea of a detour. How many times in our lives do doors slam shut, only to send us in a new direction or back to a place away from which we should have never ventured. When a door closes, it is easy to get discouraged and think that God is not working in our lives. But we cannot see the big picture. God can. He knows where every road leads. The best way to survive the disappointment of a door suddenly closing in your face is to look back and recall the times those very doors led to open ones with opportunities that were just as promising, if not better.

I'm a schoolteacher. I teach children with multiple disabilities, and, years ago, I was out with some students flying kites. It was part of our "Outdoor Experiential Education" classes where we teach the kids healthy activities, hoping to steer them away from unhealthy choices. As my fellow teacher and friend, Gina, and I were flying the kites, I said to her, "I need to go fly a kite with *my* kids." I had been so busy as a teacher and a high school basketball coach that, at that moment, I realized that maybe I need to be home more with my kids. I was spending ten hours a day with other people's children and a mere few with mine. I put one of the kites in my car with the intention to fly it with Robbie and Hailey that afternoon. Well, after school, I went to basketball practice and then dinner and homework, and the day was over. The kite sat in my car for weeks until, suddenly, a very heavy loud door came slamming shut. After eighteen years of coaching high school basketball, my alma mater—the school where my name hangs on a banner for scoring a thousand points, where I contributed to coaching several state championship teams, where my pride and spirit filled the gym—decided to replace me. They had a new coach with a new plan in mind. I was so disappointed. Basketball was such a huge part of my life, and sharing it with young people made my heart happy. I knew I belonged on the sidelines! It was where I bloomed and where *I* wanted to be! I left the athletic director's office in tears. I drove to the beach sobbing, begging God as I drove for an explanation. I could not imagine why he would take away my passion, my love, and, at that time, what *I* believed to be my purpose! I pulled up to the beach, got out of my car, and, as I came up over the dunes, what I saw broke me down and lifted me up at the same time. There was a woman on the beach with two small children. They were flying a kite. I went home and never took another coaching job. Not only did I fly that kite with my kids, but we enjoyed so many moments we would not have had if God hadn't gently close a door.

When a door swings shut, stand firm and brave, and be patient. God's hand is on the handle of another door. Leave fear, disappointment, anger and panic behind and turn yourself in the direction of hope. *Its* door is always ajar.

Proverbs 20:24 "A person's steps are directed by the Lord. How then can anyone understand their way?"

I did not feel strong or brave or patient, and I certainly did not stand firm when the word "paralyzed" pierced my heart. I headed down the hall to try to find a bathroom where I could cry and be alone, where I could fall apart without an audience. I walked down the long quiet hall, passing door after door, all closed and not a soul in sight. It must have been close to midnight by now. When I finally came to a bathroom, I went in and stood before the mirror for what seemed to be a long time, but nothing came. I was numb. When I thought I was not going to fall apart, I left the bathroom. I headed back down the long hall toward the conference room. But I only made it about three quarters of the way back when, suddenly, my knees buckled. I fell back against the wall and slid down onto the floor. I buried my face in my hands, and the only way I can describe the sound that came from me was that I wailed from the depths of my soul. My son was a quadriplegic.

Rob heard my cry and he came down the hall to retrieve the sad bundle that I was. He lifted me to my feet, wrapped his arms around me, and we cried hard together. Then, as he turned slightly to the right, I realized something. I realized that I had been all the way down that hall, but only three quarters of the way back. I realized that every door on the hall had been closed. And now, over my husband's shoulder, I am looking at the wall I fell against and slid down, noticing that the other side of that wall was the hospital chapel, and the door was wide open.

As far as I am concerned, God was reaching out His hand right then and I had a choice to make. I could remain in the hall with the wall between me and God and continue to cry, question, wonder, and eventually grow angry and resentful, or I could walk through that door and give Him my pain. I could just step in and hand it over. I could be brave and strong with Him. It was way too heavy for me to carry anyway, so why not? Why not step in and drop it into His massive lap? So I did. I walked into the chapel, gave it up, and fell back into His mighty outstretched arms. Remember, the choice is always there because God is never absent.

Psalm 138:7 "Though I walk in the midst of trouble,
you preserve me against the wrath of my enemies;
you stretch out your hand and your right hand delivers me."

Psalm 18:2 "The Lord is my rock and my fortress, and my deliverer,
my God, my strength in whom I will trust,
my shield and the horn of my salvation,
my stronghold."

Psalm 9:9 "The Lord also will be a refuge of the oppressed,
a refuge in times of trouble"

The word "refuge" in scripture is so deliberate and powerful. In the Old Testament, when the land of Canaan was divided among the tribes of Israel, each tribe received its own territory, except for the Levi. The tribe of Levi was made up of priests who were to serve the religious and spiritual needs of the other tribes, so they were scattered throughout Palestine in forty-eight cities. Six of those cities were CITIES OF REFUGE. A person who caused the death of another person could flee to one of these cities for protection from anyone who wanted to avenge the life of the person killed. In these cities, a person was protected until he received fair trial, or until the high priest of that particular city died, after which the person was free to return home protected by authorities. Since there were six of these cities, citizens living in every part of Palestine had a *refuge* that was relatively near their homes. It is clear in scripture that by referring to God as a refuge, we are told that God is where we need to be when tragedy hits, when times are hard, when life is unbearable, and when our spiritual life is being threatened. Even more importantly, it is clear that we should flee to Him quickly.

The time we spend floundering, wondering where to turn, is when doubt, loneliness, and fear creep in. These ruthless sentiments can swallow us whole and leave us never knowing the power of Christ. I'm sure the swift journey to a city of refuge was dark and frightening for the one fleeing. There were bound to be, along the way, people out to seek revenge. I would imagine one would not sleep on the way to the city, or stop to eat or talk to other travelers for fear of being killed for what he or she did. The urgency to reach safety must have consumed them because they knew that until they reached a city of refuge, death chased after them. Death to our spiritual being comes while we are away from Him

CHAPTER 3

He Provides

Within the next twenty-four hours, my eight brothers and Rob's brother were standing around Robbie's hospital bed. From Cape May Court House, New Hampshire, Vermont, Virginia, Illinois, and Texas, they traveled all night to be with Robbie by morning. My sister was camping and had yet to hear the news. My parents were still on the road returning from a trip, desperately trying to get home as quickly as possible. The rest of Rob's family was en route and anxious to help. Because Rob and I could do nothing more than love and hope and pray right then, our families took over all responsibility of talking to the doctors, collecting information, making decisions and seeing that my family and I were taken care of, especially Robbie. They went on a web search. They began networking. They asked questions and got answers. They got things done. Four days later, Robbie was taken to Jefferson Hospital in Philadelphia, Pa. where my brothers located a doctor known for his success in anterior-posterior spinal fusion, Doctor Alexander Vaccaro. "The surgery was successful."

I was never really sure why they called it "successful." My son was not fixed. He was all in one piece, but he did not work the way he had before. He could not move anything below his chest. They told me he would regain the use of his biceps and wrists, but that was it. I was not satisfied.

When I was nine, someone had given me a jewelry box. It was the kind with the little ballerina that twirled around to a sweet song when you opened it. I kept it on my dresser and one afternoon I accidently knocked it off. The ballerina broke off her stand and bounced across the hardwood floor. I immediately opened the box to make sure it stilled played and it did! So I took the broken ballerina to my dad and I asked him if he could fix it. After all, my dad could fix anything. He put her back in place and I could hardly tell she had been glued. But when he gave it back to me, he said he was sorry that it was the best he could do. My ballerina no longer twirled. It played music, but it didn't twirl. It wasn't fixed. I cried.

As my relationship with Christ matures, I realize now that it is the music that matters more than the dance. And as time passes I understand that although Robbie's body is broken, he still has an opportunity to make music. True tragedy would be for the music in a working body to die. I am grateful that he kept my son's heart beating, for it is with the heart that we produce good. Robbie's opportunity to know Christ and to create a song that will touch lives has not been taken away, but has been magnified.

**James 2:26 "For as the body without the spirit is dead,
so faith without works is dead also."**

It took two weeks in the intensive care unit before Robbie was strong enough to go to Magee Rehabilitation Hospital just blocks away, where he and I would stay for the next two months. It was there that I began keeping an online journal. Originally, the journal was set up because my dear friend Lisa knew that writing was my passion and that it would be the very ointment that could ease the pain of my burning heart. What neither of us realized, was that the journey on which I was about to embark, and the words I was about to write would do more than inform. God sent through me, words that would awaken, heal, unite, soften, enlighten, frighten, and humble. I believe He sent my son, to send me, to send you, to Him.

I have always known of Post Traumatic stress, but recently I read about something called Post Traumatic growth and it struck me because now, seven years after that tragic night, I find myself having grown and matured spiritually to the point where I am compelled to share what I have learned about life and about my God through tragedy. And so I go back into the past, into my journal, into my heart, to salvage the moments, the lessons and the words that will introduce you to the God I know and the faith that I lean on.

The difference between post traumatic stress and post traumatic growth is how we respond to our situation. There are so many things in life that can break us, so many battles that can beat us and so many thoughts that can creep in and infect our spirit. When we come up against anything in this life, we need to be prepared. We need strength, ammunition, and endurance. This translates into faith.

Philippians 4:6-7 "Do not be anxious about anything
but in every situation, by prayer and petition,
with thanksgiving let your request be made to God.
And the peace of God, which surpasses all understanding
will guard your hearts and your minds in Christ Jesus."

Journal Entry
Saturday, August 26, 2006

Today was a good day. It's been exactly a month since the injury and it was good to finally see him rest. Rob was here to help me get him up and dressed. What a difference it makes not to have to do it alone. Such is life. During one of our early morning talks toward the beginning of our journey, Robbie said to me "Mom, I just want to walk again and be able to hold Amanda's hand again." Looking at his limp fingers and his lifeless legs, I thought that might be too much to ask just yet. I thought maybe God had a plan for all this. I remembered when God was raining down manna from heaven he told the people to take enough for one day. I shared that with Robbie and told him that maybe we should just ask for enough for that day and see how it goes. He agreed and said "O.k. Today I hope to be able to stay up in the wheelchair without passing out and just to see

Amanda. That would be enough." That day, Robbie's blood pressure remained stable enough for the first time to stay up in the chair for hours, and when Amanda left that night after a nice visit, we realized that our prayers had been answered. Since then, we have had more good days than bad because we are only asking that we be given enough for a day, believing that when tomorrow comes, God will provide once again.

I wish you all enough!
Peace and Love
Sue

How often are we guilty of worrying about tomorrow, or a week from now, or even years when God himself told Moses "I will rain down bread from Heaven for you. The people are to go out and gather enough for that day." (Exodus 16:4) God was telling the people to trust him, for those who stored up had no faith. Fear, doubt and greed are the opposite of faith my friend. Remember how Jesus told us to pray? He said **"Give us this day, our *daily* bread." Matthew 6:11**

Exodus 16:4 "I will rain down bread from heaven for you.
The people are to go out and gather
enough for that day."

**Matthew 6:34 "So do not worry about tomorrow,
for tomorrow will bring worries of its own."**

Journal Entry

Monday, September 4, 2006

The other night I was chatting with one of the boys Robbie had become friends with due to similar injuries. He said something that struck me. He said "If God would just give me back the use of my hands, I would be so grateful. I would be in church every day." Although I pray for Robbie's hands to heal, I sometimes feel guilty for asking when I feel that his life itself was a gift. When do we stop asking for more? When are we satisfied? There's a man here named Jose who steers his wheelchair with his head because it's the only thing he can move, whereas Robbie steers with his arm. I wonder if Jose's prayer is "If I could only have my arms like Robbie, I'd be grateful."? Another fellow named Dave had an accident that left him not only paralyzed, but blind and with a breathing tube down his throat. Is his prayer "If I could only see and speak like Jose, I'd be grateful."? We all do it. "If only I had a little more money, or a bigger house or a better job or a nicer body or a stronger marriage or more friends ... I'd be grateful. I'd be in church every day." Why are we not in church everyday praising God for what we do have? Why do we focus on what has been taken away or never attained rather than acknowledging our creator for all that is good in our lives? Let's begin today with a prayer of gratitude. Thank God for giving my son the ability to move his arms, speak, hear, see, think, laugh and love, because that's enough for today.

I wish you enough
Peace and Love,
Sue

Stop and consider the provisions you received today and decide for yourself if it was enough. Did you have enough food? Were you warm enough? Were you clothed enough? Did you thirst for even a moment? Did you experience a loved one, laughter, a hug, a phone call? Did you have more pain than you can handle, or did you handle it? I know that some days seem overwhelming, but if you really think about what is overwhelming you, you will realize it is either the pain from yesterday or the worry about tomorrow! God provides for TODAY and He is doing that right now for you as long as you are letting Him. Take a deep breath and ask God for your "daily bread." And at the end of the day, praise Him for the delivery.

I don't know what God's plan is for my son and I don't know that it is not better than the route my son was about to choose, so I'm going to trust and not question. I don't know where my son was heading at age sixteen. I don't know that he was not going to jump in a van with his guitar in hand and run off to California and get mixed up with a bad crowd and end up in a bad place. I don't know that! Yes, there may be a worse place than a wheelchair and perhaps, just perhaps my God was protecting my son from something worse. I can think this way because **Romans 8:28 says "We know in all things, God works for the good of those who love him, who have been called according to his purpose."** So how can I question where my God has placed me *or* my son? Life sends us to places we don't want to go. It sends us down paths where the road signs read "pain," "fear," "embarrassment," "humility," "loneliness," etc. and when we come to one of these, we pray and we beg not to have to go. But I'm learning that rather than ask God *not* to send me, it makes more sense to ask Him to go *with* me. I cannot help but remember that God is good all the time, so if He is asking you to go down a path with a sign that reads something frightening like CANCER, there may be something down that path you need to experience to become who God intended you to be. So go! Just ask Him to go with you, and each day pray for what you need for that day. Ask God to give you strength to withstand the treatments, love to carry you from morning to night, laughter just because it feels good, courage to go where you don't want to go, and—more than anything— faith in Him who has promised to never leave you. (Hebrews 13:5) And when He wakes you with another day, simply reach out and take His hand again and He will lead you safely to another sunset. I honestly believe that we are like clay figures here on earth and our experiences are God's hands at work. If we not only accept, but also embrace those experiences He puts before us, around us and inside us: if we listen, learn, and trust that God is in control, then His hands will mold us, shape us, and perfect us. And over time—God's time—we develop into exactly what He envisioned when He plucked a wad of clay and gave it our name. If we try to fashion the wad ourselves, we will fail. I don't know what Robbie will look like when the Master's hands finally rest, but I know that God is always working on him, in him, and through him. And I know that there is no greater artist, so it will be wonderful.

Proverbs 3:5-6 "Trust in the Lord with all your heart,
lean not on your own understanding.
In all your ways acknowledge him
and he will make your path straight."

The scripture reads "ALL your heart," "ALL your ways." It doesn't say SOME of your heart and A FEW of your ways, but ALL. In this earthly life, it is very difficult to walk a straight path, for the distractions are many. We are distracted by what *we* want, rather than focused on God's will. A straight path is one that centers on our maker, not us. By trusting God and including Him in everything you do, He will lead you forward and guard you from distractions. He will clear your path.

CHAPTER 4

The Gift of People

A nother amazing gift my God provides is others. When I talk about sharing our journey with the people with whom we have been blessed, I cannot say enough. If you really pay attention, you can go back and find a perfect specific "good" purpose for every individual who has appeared in your life story. Think about it ... the nice, the mean, the sad, the happy, the jealous, the good and even the bad people have added to the ingredients of you. I think it is pretty cool and I know it is on purpose, so try not to turn anyone away. When we come to realize we are all here for each other, we are going to do some amazing things.

John 13:34 "Love one another."

Journal Entry
August 28, 2006

Upon our return from Robbie's doctor's appointment, we sat on the roof together and enjoyed the fresh air. As I looked over the city from six stories up, I saw life buzzing on. People were rushing from place to place, talking on cell phones, crossing against traffic lights because something couldn't wait, discussing business on lunch breaks, and shopping for things nobody really needs. People were running, horns were beeping, vendors were hustling, etc. Suddenly, I realized that life had stopped for me—but, as I turned back to Robbie, it sobered me to the reality that nothing down there matters: jobs, money, cars, time, clothing, jewelry, plans, promotions, impressions ... nothing, except the people. They matter. The people we encounter every second of our lives ... from our dearest family and friends to the guy sleeping in the alley that made me feel grateful for the chair on which I've been sleeping.. The way our community has gathered in my family's behalf is a prime example of what matters. Life is about our travel companions and, when we leave here, we leave everything below the roof down on the street and take along everything that grew in us from others. So because of the people in my life, I feel very wealthy.

I wish you enough
Peace and Love,
Sue

I took Hailey to the orthodontist a few months after Robbie and I returned home from the hospital. Dr. Jeff Vecere took such amazing care of Hailey. He had to put a device on one of her teeth to guide it into place. Then he put braces on her teeth and followed up with her care until the day she had them removed years later. Because he understood what our medical bills were mounting up to, he did it all free of charge. He gifted my daughter with a beautiful smile. I was so grateful and even more amazed with his response to my gratitude. "I've been blessed," he said. "This is what I do, and it is what I have to offer." It says in the Bible—in **1 Peter 4:10** "Like good stewards of the manifold grace of God, serve one another with whatever gift each of you has received." In other words, recognize that you have been blessed, fine-tune your gifts, and use them for good. It also says in **1 Peter 4:11:** "If anyone ministers, let him do it as with the ability which God supplies." How many of us are doing just that? How many of us use our gifts to make money, to make friends, to make a name for ourselves? How many of us use our gifts to make a *difference*? Most of all, how many of us use the gifts that God gave us to glorify Him? He is the one who stocked our toolboxes. He is the one who shaped our hands and filled our minds. He is the ink in our pens, the desire in our hearts, and the good in every good thing that comes through us. Take your gift (and everyone has one) and do something great with it, as Jeff Vecere did. Share, give, help, heal, lift, comfort, provide, save.

In looking back, I am amazed and grateful for whom God put into place prior to sending me on this journey. It took my maker forty-three years to paint the details into the scene that would be my life when tragedy hit. Everything and everyone was in place when God said, "Action!" I've heard people in the midst of disaster say, "Nothing can prepare you for something like this." My husband was feeling just that on September 23, 2006.

Sue Wunder

Journal Entry
September 23, 2006

While Rob and I were eating dinner and reflecting on the past two months,
he lifted his head and gazed out the window into the city streets and said,
"Nothing could have prepared us for something like this."

But the truth is we could not have been better prepared. I said to him,
"Think about it. What do we need that we don't have to get through this?"
Nothing. It occurred to me that God had prepared us and that he was very
generous in providing us with the ammunition needed to battle this beast.
He gave us a supportive, loving family with parents who taught us
sacrifice and unconditional love. He put us in a profession that taught us
about patience and tolerance, a job that taught us compassion and made
us sensitive to the smallest of miracles. We are in an occupation
surrounded by qualified professionals who have become friends. There are
physical therapists, occupational therapists, psychologists, and social
workers willing to help. He led us to be athletes and coaches, where we
learned to motivate, support and to get up each time we fell. He gathered
a group of friends and a community around us that he knew would carry
us when this happened. And because of all this, He's given me faith in His
love and His word. I want for nothing today, for I know that we have been
clad with God's gifts. I suppose it was why David turned down King Saul's

offer of a helmet and armor to fight Goliath. God had already dressed him in faith.

I wish you enough
Peace and Love,
Sue

1 Samuel 17:34-37 "But David said to Saul, 'Your servant has been keeping his father's sheep. When a lion or a bear came and carried off a sheep from the flock, I went after it, struck it and rescued the sheep from its mouth.

When it turned on me, I seized it by its hair, struck it and killed it. Your servant has killed both the lion and the bear; this uncircumcised Philistine (Goliath) will be like one of them, because he has defied the armies of the living God.

The Lord who rescued me from the paw of the lion and the paw of the bear will rescue me from the hand of this Philistine.'"

It is interesting that when King Saul told David he was too small to fight Goliath, David relied on his past experiences and how God looked after him and his sheep. He had killed lions and bears and God protected him through each encounter. He had faith that God would protect him now against Goliath, and it was that faith that made him strong enough to slay the giant. It would do us well when we have a question as to whether God will bring us through something, to look back. Is there anything in your life you have already survived? That was God. Is there a moment you can remember when you thought there was no hope and yet hope arrived? That was God. Is there a person who was there for you that kept you from curling up in a ball and giving up? That was God! He does provide! He not only places people strategically to support and encourage, but to teach us the things that matter. He sends them in the midst of their own experience for us to witness, to pay attention, and to take notes on subjects like generosity, gratitude, compassion, patience, and love.

CHAPTER 5

Lessons Learned

GENEROSITY
(A third grader)

Journal Entry
December 18, 2006

Robbie was invited as the guest of honor at a holiday show at Middle Township Elementary School. We entered the auditorium where the entire third, fourth, and fifth grade student body had gathered. They reserved an area front and center for our family. We listened to the choir. It was so nice. There is just something about the holiday songs when they come from children. I think it is because the spirit of the holidays is still fresh in them. The wonder and the realness of the magic is still in the air that they breathe. So much of that fizzles out by the time we are adults, as the true meaning of the holidays fades into the background of shopping malls, rush orders, last minute crafts, and forced entertaining. But the children sang from that place in their new hearts where no adult could ever go to muster up tunes like we heard today. It was beautiful. After the singing, the principals presented Robbie with a 1600 dollar check the school had raised on his behalf. It was wonderful! But just when I thought I had seen God as much as I was going to in this day, a very small third grader walked up to me after the auditorium had emptied and she tapped me on the hip. I turned and looked down at this tiny little girl as she stretched toward me a closed fist. I opened my palm to receive what seemed to be a gift offering. And when her little hand opened, a quarter, a dime, a nickel, and seven pennies jingled into my hand. Forty-seven cents she gave me. I'm guessing it was everything she had. I will forever cherish the gifts of that day, large and small.

I wish you enough
Peace and Love,
Sue

Luke 6:38 "Give, and it will be given to you.
Good measure, pressed down, shaken together, running over,
will be put into your lap. For with the measure you use
it will be measured back to you."

Luke 21:1-4 "Jesus looked up and saw the rich
putting their gifts into the offering box,
and he saw a poor widow put in two small copper coins.
And he said, "Truly, I tell you, this poor widow
has put in more than all of them.
For they all contributed out of their abundance,
but she out of her poverty put in all she had to live on."

Journal Entry
October 27, 2006

Rob came home from work yesterday with a note from a fellow teacher. Her husband Larry works in the sod business and has a group of men working for him. They do not make much and send a good portion of their salaries to their families in Mexico. The other day, while they were working, one of the men asked Larry what the bracelet on his wrist meant. He said it was a "Root For Robbie" bracelet that he bought for two dollars to support Robbie, and he told his workers about Robbie's situation. Each of the guys bought a bracelet, and one of them bought an extra one to send home to his wife. Two days later—it was payday—the guys approached Larry with a folded piece of paper. They said it was for Robbie. When he opened it, there were eight precious dollars for my son. I was so moved. I am amazed how a tragedy can go so deep into the human spirit and well up such pure love and generosity from the bottom of the human heart.

I wish you enough
Peace and Love,
Sue

Sue Wunder

GRATITUDE
(The Donut Shop Man)

Journal Entry
February 13, 2006

I'm counting on a phone call tomorrow to tell me to stay in my warm bed and rest because the world outside is covered with snow. I can't help but think of a man, though. I passed him every day on my walk through the city to where I was offered a warm shower at the home of some kind folks. But this man ignited the gratitude in me not by giving, but by needing. He was old and tired, dirty and quiet, and he sat just outside the donut shop looking for handouts. I gave him a few bucks the first time I saw him, and he nodded with a shy "Thank you." But each day after that, I passed and he never put his hand out. I could see him look up and notice me coming, but still, he would put down his head and I think he was hoping. I gave him enough for breakfast each time I passed and I watched him go into the store anxious to eat. I think he started to count on me. Then I left, came home to my warm house, my loving family, a town full of love and friends, a good job, a cozy bed, and plenty of food. The donut shop man, though, is still there I believe, on the corner, in the city, in the cold, hoping for enough for his day. I hope he is warm tonight, and fed. I love him for magnifying my gratitude.

I wish you enough
Peace and Love,
Sue

32

**1 Thessalonians 5:18 "Give thanks in all circumstances;
for this is the will of God in Christ Jesus for you."**

**James 1:2-3 "Consider it pure joy, my brothers and sisters,
whenever you face trials of many kinds,
because you know that the testing of your faith
produces perseverance."**

COMPASSION

(A stranger's whisper)

Journal Entry
September 15, 2006

I went across the street tonight to retrieve dinner for myself, Robbie, Hailey, and Rob and, as I waited for the food, I lay my head down on the table. I dozed off quickly just for a moment and a man approached me. Without knowing my situation, he leaned down and whispered in my ear, "Your load will lighten up. God never gives us more than we can handle." I lifted my head and he was gone. That was a wonderful act of kindness to simply remind me that God is aware and here. I continue to be amazed at human kindness lately. I don't know. Before this happened, I was beginning to notice a weakening population as far as faith, selflessness, and compassion are concerned. I was seeing more greed than giving. I was witnessing more tension than understanding, and I was hearing more anger in voices than love. But now, I see it like a rose among weeds. In the midst of darkness, a light in the form of true human kindness shines. There is love and compassion and generosity flourishing here on earth. Sometimes we just get so distracted that God has to holler to get our attention and to bring us back to our intended form—love. Sometimes, if we are lucky, he only has to whisper.

I wish you enough
Peace and Love,
Sue

Galatians 6:2 "Carry each other's burdens,
and in this way you will fulfill the law of Christ."

Luke 10:30 In reply Jesus said: "A man was going down from Jerusalem to Jericho, when he was attacked by robbers. They stripped him of his clothes, beat him and went away, leaving him half dead. A priest happened to be going down the same road, and when he saw the man, he passed by on the other side. So too, a Levite, when he came to the place and saw him, passed by on the other side. But a Samaritan, as he traveled, came where the man was; and when he saw him, he took pity on him. He went to him and bandaged his wounds, pouring on oil and wine. Then he put

the man on his own donkey, brought him to an inn and took care of him. The next day he took out two denarii and gave them to the innkeeper. 'Look after him,' he said, 'and when I return, I will reimburse you for any extra expense you may have. "Which of these three do you think was a neighbor to the man who fell into the hands of robbers?" The expert in the law replied, "The one who had mercy on him." Jesus told him, "Go and do likewise."

When I consider the other people in the restaurant that night and the fact that others must have noticed me asleep on the table, I realize that this man who had enough mercy on me to stop and whisper in my ear was a "neighbor" to me as he acted just the way Jesus expects us to act. We should all consider our own behavior when we do not take time to stop and listen or give someone a ride or loan someone money or feed someone or just give out of love. We see someone hitchhiking and we are afraid they might hurt us so we do not pick them up. We see someone intoxicated on the street who needs money but we assume he or she would buy alcohol so we do not share. We see someone who is hungry but he or she is very dirty and we are afraid we may get sick, so we keep our distance. We are all guilty of it. Life is so fast and so busy, we are all focused on our own needs, our own desires, our own futile finish lines.

PATIENCE AND LOVE
(My Daughter)

Journal Entry
September 18, 2006

Last night, I was feeding Robbie some Chinese food at 8:00 P.M., telling him we had yet to take a shower, when the phone rang. Hailey was calling to go over her homework with me. "Mom, I wrote directions on how to make a peanut butter sandwich. Do you want me to read it to you?"

I said, "Yes, of course."

She started with "Number one, slide the peanut butter jar over to you." With that, I asked in a rather weary voice how many steps she had. "Fifty-seven," she replied proudly.

Immediately, I went back to the days of being twelve and writing poetry. Every time I wrote a poem, I would go to my parents and ask if they wanted to hear it, and, every time, they did. I'd stand proudly before them with so much energy and excitement. Only now do I realize how often they must have been tired or busy or preoccupied and yet, they put aside whatever it was, and they listened. And when I finished my proud recital, I would look up for their approval. Every time, they were still looking, still listening and smiling like I had written an award-winning piece. So I listened and commented on all fifty-seven steps as I noted the pride in Hailey's voice. As tired as I was, I knew right then that I would be fine. All I have to do is love like I have been loved. Thanks, Hailey, for opening my eyes.

I wish you enough.
Peace and love
Sue

I often wonder how many opportunities and lessons we miss because we are not paying attention to whom God places in front of us, or because we are too busy or too tired or too focused on something other than Him. We tend to make plans and stick to them. We have places to go, things to do, and people to see. I wonder how many *I* missed. Was there someone I did not make time for who needed to say something to me or show me something? Did I turn away from opportunities to grow? Did I avoid or ignore someone who was carrying in him or her a valuable lesson for me? I am sure.

37

CHAPTER 6

When God Sends Us

T he other idea we need to consider is that we must not only become more aware of the people God sends to us, but become conscious of the fact that He sends us to others! Oftentimes, our activities or actions make a difference in someone's life and we never know about it. I was blessed to find out about a life God saved using me.

I was at a party and a woman approached me. She said, "Hi, Sue, I know we have met, but I have a story I have never had the opportunity to share with you."

I said, "Great!"

She continued, "When your son was injured, you began to write a journal online and a friend of mine turned me on to it. I read it every day and I prayed for Robbie. I loved the things that you wrote and your faith was contagious. Two months after Robbie was injured, my five-year-old son was hit by a drunk driver. He was in a coma and I was told after several weeks that he would not wake. I was on the roof of the hospital falling apart and I wanted to end my life. I did not want to live another day without my son. Then I thought of you and your faith and your strength and I thought, "I need to go back to reading that journal." I came down from the roof and I began reading again about hope and strength and God, and I just want you to know that when my son *did* wake up seven months later, I was there for him because of you." Wow! That was not because of me, my friends. That was because God can and does use us for His purpose. I will be forever grateful to God for revealing that story to me and for reminding me that we can't see the whole picture. We don't know what God is doing but we have to know it is always good.

Just as this woman reflected on my faith and my obedience, I reflected on the obedience of the Virgin Mary one morning over coffee and wrote her a letter.

Journal Entry
November 10, 2006

Dear Mary –

I am writing to you, from mother to mother, because I need some strength from you. I read about your suffering and I watched a reenactment of the day your heart was torn from your chest, flogged, mocked, nailed to a cross and left to thirst, then die. I wish I could have been there to comfort you, or even cry with you. From what I read, you were amazing. Your strength and faith in God carries me now. With all you had to lose by becoming pregnant as a virgin, you still said yes to God. You risked disaster! You risked remaining unmarried for life. You risked your own father's rejection and the possibility of being forced into begging or prostitution in order to earn a living. You risked being called crazy with a story about being made pregnant by the Holy Spirit. When Gabriel came to you, you had no idea he was offering you a great opportunity. You only knew that God was asking you to serve, and you said yes! No questions asked. "May it be to me as you have said" were your words according to Luke. Wow! You have taught me so much Mary. By your example, I've learned that even when the outcome seems disastrous, we still need to offer ourselves willingly to God. It's really a hard thing to do sometimes, especially when it involves our child, our heart, and soul. Especially when we're surrounded by unbelievers in this world. Yea, I know how Sarah laughed and Abraham doubted, and yet you submitted. What faith! I wish you were here in my kitchen, Mary, having coffee with me, so that I could look into your eyes and see the peace I'm searching for now. But even though we are hundreds of generations apart, I feel such a connection to you and your son, Jesus. This is God's amazing, constant hand through time. And even though no angel spoke to me about this event, I do accept it as God's purpose and His will. And I think of you every day, Mary, and how you said to Elizabeth, "My soul glorifies the Lord and my spirit rejoices in God my Savior, for He has been mindful of the humble state of His servant." You did good, Mary. I hope I can serve as well.

I wish you enough
peace and love,
Sue

Mary reminds us to be obedient and to trust even though we do not understand the how, when, or why of a situation. It is oftentimes difficult to make sense of where we are or what we are looking at. But there is comfort in knowing it is where we belong simply because we believe that God is the master planner.

Journal Entry
September 2, 2006

The boys all gathered in our room for a movie today. It was cozy and there's nothing like a comedy on a rainy day. Robbie has formed some unique friendships here and it's a beautiful thing. He, Tariq, John, Kyle, and Pat sat in a circle today, each one lounged back in a tilt, just chatting. "Can you feel this?" "Can you do that?" "Do your legs spasm?" "Do you have triceps?" "Let me see your scar." "Do you think we'll ever walk again?" I thought, God, It's not supposed to be like this. *It should be "Do you play ball?" "You like rap?" "What kind of car you driving?" "Where you going to college?" And I labored to make sense of it, to find something right there in that picture that would explain why. Then I realized that those five boys were on one puzzle piece of God's enormous puzzle and, without the box lid, there is no way we are going to comprehend His masterpiece. Imagine, though, if we had God's box lid, we could see the whole beautiful picture and celebrate our little piece and how perfectly it fits in. Hey, look! I'm the blue in a rainbow! Wow! I'm the petal of a flower! This thing I'm going through ... it's the spot on a butterfly's wing that keeps it from getting eaten by its predator! We could make sense of it! Well, we don't have the box lid, but we should have faith that works just as well. And I believe that when you let go of what you think it should look like, God smiles as He presses the piece that fits you neatly into His masterpiece. So, you see, we need to stop being afraid simply because we don't understand and rejoice in the fact that we don't have to.*

I wish you enough
Peace and Love,
Sue

**Proverbs 3:5 "Trust in the LORD with all your heart
and lean not on your own understanding."**

CHAPTER 7

Trusting God

One morning a few months later, as I was trusting God and leaning not on my own narrow field of vision, God expanded the lens and comforted me with a slightly larger picture, one that provided me with an opportunity to contemplate the gift rather than the loss.

Journal Entry
December 9, 2006

I read a story in the press today about a postal woman who was hit by a car months ago. Her husband and I crossed paths quite often at Magee. I was in the elevator with him one morning when he said to me, "Today I have to tell her she's lost both her legs." My heart sank. Here was a woman who had already lost her sight and lay in bed thinking her legs were only injured. Now, she was going to learn that her legs had been amputated. And today in the newspaper several months later, she is quoted as saying "I'll be okay." Amazing. But when you see a bigger picture, things become clearer. Imagine standing outside Magee hospital on a cool September night, looking up through the illuminated windows. Robbie sits in his wheelchair on the fifth floor, paralyzed from the chest down, but looking out the window at the bluest of skies. He's laughing with his friends and listening to music. Just below him on the fourth floor, Maureen lies in bed with no legs at all and eyes that see only darkness, but she smiles and speaks with her husband, enjoys his company, and assures him that she will be okay. Just below her on the third floor is a young man named James who cannot speak or move and gives no indication that he can even hear because of his brain injury. James is pushed down the hall by his mother who stares into space wondering where her son has gone. If you stand outside this building looking into the three windows at once, Robbie's future looks the brightest. He was given the gift of sight, hearing, speech, a whole body, and a healthy brain. The more of the picture you see my friend, the easier it is to comprehend.

I wish you enough
Peace and Love,
Sue

1 Corinthians 13:12 "For now we see only a reflection as in a mirror;
Then we shall see face to face. Now I know in part;
Then I shall know fully, even as I am fully known."

Believing in what we cannot see is a difficult thing, especially when what we do see makes little sense. It requires trust and a letting go of fear. It requires faith. Faith is defined as **"being sure of what we hope for and certain of what we do not see." (Hebrews 11:1)** A friend of mine told me once that I had the *gift* of faith. As I began to wonder how that gift was delivered, I began to contemplate the relationship I have with my own parents. Having grown up with eight boys, I ran to my mom and dad every time I was teased, pinched, injured during a rough game, or brokenhearted when they wouldn't let me play. My parents comforted me. I remember curling up on my dad's lap and crying into his shirt. They also provided for me. Every meal we ever ate, my mother never fixed her plate until everyone's was full. She made sure we were fed first. As I grew older, I sat and talked with them about school or my occupation and they helped me make decisions. I always trusted their advice because time and time again it proved to work. As the years went by, I went to Mom and Dad for advice on raising children and handling finances. I would share my fears and celebrate my triumphs around that kitchen table that saw and heard so much.

Today, my parents are my earthly support. If anything were to fall apart, they stand waiting to pick up the pieces. They call every other day to ask how my family is doing and want to know if we need anything. When I give them good news, they cry with joy. My mom and dad *cry* for me and my family because they love us so much. Since Robbie's injury, there has been financial strain. My parents have paid for repairs of our truck, a new roof on our house, college tuition for our children, gas in our cars, and even after all of that, they send a check every spring called "a spring booster" just in case we fall behind. My mom and my dad have taught me through their actions what it means to love a child unconditionally. They showed me that a parent's love is boundless. They put me in the mind frame not to stress about money or decisions or family because if it is something I cannot handle financially, emotionally or strategically, I would never be alone because they will be there to help. THAT is how we should view our Father in Heaven, for we are His.

Galatians 3:26 "So in Christ Jesus you are all
children of God through faith."

John 1:12 "But to all who did receive him,
who believed in his name,
he gave the right to become children of God."

1 John 3:1 "See what great love the Father has lavished on us,
that we should be called children of God! And that is what we are!"

If my earthly parents can demonstrate such love and devotion, I can only imagine what my heavenly Father is capable of! By painting me a picture of love, my parents showed me who God is. **God *is* love. (1 John 4:7-8)** As I came to know God and formed an intimate relationship with Him through His word, I realized that He too will be there when I am in need. He too will comfort and provide and no matter what, love me, simply because I am His. I need not worry about anything because I have HIM. Faith grows in many people through their experiences. Others seek it and find it through studying the word. Still others have had it, but lost it when times were hard. For me, faith was a gift God explained to me through my parents. A gift that I will forever cherish. A gift that gives me comfort and peace. It is a gift that lets me rest in Him when I would otherwise be unable to rest.

2 Corinthians 5:6-7 "Therefore we are always confident and know that as long as we are at home in the body, we are away from the Lord, for we live by faith not by sight."

2 Timothy 1:7 "For the Spirit God gave us does not make us timid, but gives us power, love and self discipline."

Journal Entry
October 10, 2006

It's 11:00 pm and I'm afraid now that we are home from the hospital and Robbie's care is up to us. He's downstairs and I sleep upstairs. I have a monitor, but what if I don't hear him? I did his bowel routine at 10:00 but he didn't go yet. What if he doesn't go? I have a timer to wake me at 1:00, 3:00, and 5:00, but what if I don't hear that? What if the electricity goes out or the batteries don't work? I have to empty his bladder at 1:00 and 5:00. What if he only goes 100 cc's the first time? What if it's over 500 cc's? He went to bed shivering so I bundled him up. What if he gets hot and can't take the blankets down? What if I don't hear him when he needs a drink or his pillow flipped or his foot rubbed or his leg stretched? What if I don't do it all just right? What if? Maybe I should blow up the air mattress I had pressed into the hospital chair and lay it down on his floor by his bed. I could be right there like I'd been all along. Then I'd be sure to hear him and I could keep him safe. Or ... maybe I'll pull the blankets up to his chin, kiss him on the forehead, turn out his light, go upstairs, get into my bed, and as I close my eyes to rest, hand it over to God. I could ask Him to keep watch while I rest. Yea, that's what I'll do, tonight and from now on. I'll put my faith in God.

I wish you enough
Peace and Love,
Sue

Psalm 56:3 "When I am afraid, I put my trust in you."

Psalm 84:12 "O LORD Almighty, blessed is the man who trusts in you."

Romans 15:13 "May the God of hope fill you with all joy and peace as you trust in him, so that you may overflow with hope by the power of the Holy Spirit."

How many times a year, a month, a week, a day, a *minute,* do you have to turn your worries over to God? Even worse is how many times you choose *not* to hand it over, but to hold on to it, to control it, and to believe that you know what is best. It seems to me every time I think I know how things should go and I grab the wheel and start steering, I usually end up at a dead end on my knees praying after all. Why do we insist on giving it the old college try? When it does not work out, only then do we begin to beg our God to come to our rescue. If you and a friend had to cross a river and you knew it would be easy if you simply held hands, would you tell your friend, "Let me try it on my own and if I fall in, come save me and we will go from there." No! You would take your friend's hand and cross. We need to know that on the bank of ever river standing next to us is our God with His hand outstretched. Reach first, *then* cross. When we step forward in faith rather than fear, our experience is bound to be the one that He intended for us rather than the one we fathomed on our own.

Letting go of fear and grabbing on to faith changes every experience we have. When I was little, my dad took me out into the ocean where it was over my head. I was frightened, but I wrapped my arms around his neck and held on tight. I told him I was scared and he said, "It's okay, I'm not going to let go of you." And I believed him. Once I realized I was safe in his arms, I embraced the experience and let the huge waves wash over me. We laughed and challenged each on as it came. I felt the waves, I tasted the salt, and, without fear, I covered a tiny portion of life's journey. When we got back to shore, I was different from that experience, even as a small child. And as we get older, our experiences get bigger and more challenging, but they still serve the same purpose—to make us different, more whole, more finished, and with more faith in the one holding us. So, no matter what you might be going through, wrap your arms around your Heavenly Father, and know that He will not let go of you. Take on the waves! Laugh at the big ones! Let life wash right over you! And know that when you get back to shore, you will not only be different, but you will still be in the arms of your Father.

Faith strengthens with spiritual maturity, and spiritual maturity comes by way of different avenues. You might choose to grow closer to God by studying His word or joining a Bible group. You may choose to attend church every week and spend quality time contemplating the message. You may choose to take time out to simply be alone with Him in prayer and listening. Then there are those of us who, in the midst of a "lazy" spiritual life, have God step in and open our eyes, fine-tune our hearing, and tenderize our hearts by allowing an experience to wake us spiritually to the sound of His voice. I am not saying that if you do not pay attention to God, He is going to wake you with a tragic event. But I am saying that if He needs to use you for His glory or needs your attention for a reason you may never know, He *will* call.

CHAPTER 8

Where Was God?

I have seen God use Robbie so many times since the incident, but never once did I believe that it was God's hand that hurt Robbie in order to glorify Himself. That is not how our Father works. God is good ALL THE TIME. ONLY good flows from His being. Knowing that, I can visualize where my maker's hand was the night Robbie was injured. A couple of weeks after Robbie and I came home from the hospital, a woman stopped by my house. She said to me, "You don't know me, but I heard about Robbie and your journal and I've been reading and praying for you and your family. I stopped by to ask you something." She continued "How have you maintained your faith when God has allowed such a tragedy in your life?" Wow! I never really considered what happened that night as a result of God's apathy. I celebrate what happened that night because of His *action*. Robbie did not dive into the pool and break his neck because God let him fall. He survived the incident because God lifted him up! When tragedy hits, people often ask the question, "Why does God allow bad things to happen? Why didn't He create a world where tragedy and suffering do not exist?" God did create a perfect world! **Genesis 1:31** tells us that **"God saw all that He had made and it was very good."** God is love, and when He decided to create us, I'm sure

He wanted us to experience love, but to give us the ability to love, He had to give us free will so we could *decide* whether to love or not. It would be our choice. We as humans have abused our free will by turning away from God, and so introducing evil into the world. I am sure God knew this would happen because God knows everything, but think of it this way: If you have children, before you had them, didn't you anticipate the possibility that they might suffer disappointment or pain or heartache in life? Did you consider the fact that they might even turn away from you and hurt you? I am sure these things crossed your mind, but you still had children because you knew there was also the potential for joy, deep love, and tremendous meaning. God sympathizes with us. If you put your trust in Him, He is in you and your suffering is His suffering. So when tragedy strikes—and it will because Jesus said in **John 16:33 "In this world you will have trouble"**—run to your Father, for in His arms you will find peace for today and courage to face tomorrow.

Jeremiah 29:11 "For I know the plans I have for you, declares the Lord,
plans to prosper you and not to harm you,
plans to give you hope and a future."

Psalm 121: 1-8 "I lift up my eyes to the mountains.
Where does my help come from?
My help comes from the Lord, the Maker of heaven and earth.

He will not let your foot slip; he who watches

over you will not slumber;

indeed, he who watches over Israel will neither slumber nor sleep.

The Lord watches over you. The Lord is your shade at your right hand,

the sun will not harm you by day, nor the moon by night;

The Lord will keep you from all harm;

The Lord will watch over your life;

the Lord will watch over your coming and going both now and

forevermore."

So you see, God does answer. He does rescue, protect, deliver, satisfy, and watch over us. God provides for us. We have to notice God's work, the things He gives, and praise Him for it. When something hurts, praise God for what does *not* hurt. When something is lost, praise God for what we still have! When someone is gone, praise God for the time you had with them. There is power in praise! I have felt it! So often we go to God with a list of requests without first remembering to thank and praise. Let us not forget that when Jesus was teaching His disciples how to pray, the Lord's prayer did not begin with "Give us this day...." It begins with "Our father who art in Heaven, hallowed be thy name." The word "hallowed" means sanctified or separate from us and holy. We are to first glorify His name and praise Him. "Thy kingdom come, thy will be done" tells us to honor God's will before our own, to forfeit our wishes to His will. Only then, after we have praised and submitted to His will, do we make our requests known to God. I might also repeat that the "request" part of the prayer does not go beyond "Daily" bread. So when we come to God and as we slip into a pew at church, let us be reminded that it is not about us, but about Him.

Journal Entry
November 12, 2006

We went to church as a family today. It was not the church I was used to going to, as we were invited by friends to attend their service. Different building, different people, different songs, same God. And since my goal was to worship, it was just right. I was reminded today what attending church is all about. Too often, we go to church to feel good, to pray for ourselves or others, to "put in our time" with God, to seek answers in scripture, for direction, for belonging, for solace, for peace. But God! We have to remember that we go there for Him! We are so needy as a people that we tend to go to God more often to get than to give. I was so filled with gratitude today because Robbie was sitting there beside me. I thank God every day that He didn't take Robbie on July 23, 2006. No, He didn't take him, He changed him. And only God knows why. And even though I don't understand it, I have to believe that the change was a necessary stroke of God's brush for the perfection of His work. I know it was. I trust Him. If you are wondering how a mother can sit in church beside her son who has lost his ability to walk, use his hands, to enjoy his passion (guitar) etc., and still praise the God who gives and takes away, well, I will tell you. The friend sitting beside me lost her son less than a year ago and she was there to worship the same Father who let me keep mine. That is faith, trust, and love. Thanks Anne.

I wish you enough
peace and love,
Sue

Isaiah 25:1 "O Lord, you are my God; I will exalt you, I will give thanks to your name; For you have worked wonders, plans formed long ago, with perfect faithfulness."

Psalm 105: 1-2 "Give praise to the LORD, proclaim his name; make known among the nations what he has done. Sing to him, sing praise to him; tell of all his wonderful acts."

There is an amazing motivational speaker named Nick Vujicic who was born with no limbs. Imagine it: He has devoted his life to praising and glorifying God. He has shared his testimony thousands of times on God's behalf. In one of his presentations, he talked about the fact that God may not change your circumstances, and made it clear that if he did not change your situation, then He would use it. Unfortunate things happen every day to almost every person at some time or another.

Be comforted however, that God knows what to do with those unfortunate circumstances. Sometimes, using them proves to be way more powerful than changing them.

Maybe you have heard of the story of David and Bathsheba. (**2 Samuel 11**) King David noticed Bathsheba, the wife of Uriah the Hittite, from the roof of his palace one night and sent for her. He slept with her and she became pregnant. So that he and Bathsheba could be together, he sent Uriah to the front line of battle so that he would be killed. This was a terrible situation that involved adultery and murder. God did not change who David was, but he used his imperfections and his sinful heart to bring into the world the baby who would be known as King Solomon. Solomon's wisdom made him the most powerful king of his time, reigning for forty years and building the first temple in Jerusalem.

God has yet to change Robbie's circumstance as far as physical healing is concerned, but every day we see him using it to impact the lives of others, to bring love to light and to connect us to one another.

Journal Entry
October 29, 2006

A woman I did not know came by today. She presented me with a basket of gifts. She also gave me two inspirational CD's and a letter. She told me how we were "connected" through a friend of a friend and how she'd been reading my daily posts. She explained how our paths had actually crossed once on the basketball court some twenty-five years ago. She told me she has two children of her own and how they have been praying for Robbie every night, and she thanked me for my "obedience" to God. What I find so amazing is that twenty-five years ago, we shared a court. We ran past each other back and forth, back and forth, never speaking. She was blue and white. I was orange and black. I was a number. She was a number. And we spent thirty-two minutes together many times, on the same floor, loving the same thing, after the same goal, but NOT on the same team. And now, as we have grown into adults and have raised our families in different towns, our kids in different schools, have gone to different churches, suddenly she's standing in my house sharing one thing we have always had in common—GOD. What else could have brought her into my living room from so "far away" and placed us side by side on the SAME TEAM after all these years? I wish people understood just how connected we all are. God didn't hand out uniforms or numbers. He didn't divide us into varsity and junior varsity. He didn't make cuts. He didn't even make us try out! He invited us and all we have to do is say yes. When my new friend Dorann left my house, I opened the letter and folded in the pages was five one hundred dollar bills with a note signed by "Your brothers and sisters in Christ."

I wish you enough
Peace and Love,
Sue

Deuteronomy 15:7 "If anyone is poor among your fellow Israelites in any of the towns of the land the Lord your God is giving you, do not be hardhearted or tightfisted toward them. rather, be openhanded and freely lend them whatever they need."

Note that the scripture says "whatever they need." The Greek word for "poor" is *ptochos* and the definition includes "reduced to begging" and "destitute in wealth," but there is more. It also includes "destitute of the Christian virtues," "helpless," and "lacking in anything." Recognizing when someone is poor is not just looking at his or her financial situation. When the stranger noticed me with my head down on the table, he did not know my story and he did not need to know, but he knew I was "lacking" in something and he was right. I was lacking in stamina. Dorann did not know my financial situation but she knew there had to be hospital bills, time out of work, and future accommodations for Robbie. The gift of money was quite helpful, but the reminder that we have "brothers and sisters in Christ" provides even more strength and hope when we find ourselves "lacking."

Ephesians 4:2 "Be completely humble and gentle, be patient, bearing with one another in love."

Galatians 6:2 "Carry each other's burdens and in this way you will fulfill the law of Christ."

**Matthew 5:41 "If anyone forces you to go one mile,
go with him two miles."**

Journal Entry
September 19, 2006

Yesterday, there was a photo of Robbie on the bed, of him playing guitar. He asked me to pick it up and place it in his hand. I slid it between his thumb and forefinger and I watched him. His eyes studied it. As he held it, I could tell he was trying to move his fingers, but nothing came. I could see sadness, and as the corners of his mouth dipped, my heart sank for him. I had absolutely nothing to offer but a kiss on the forehead and a prayer. I could always fix everything until now. I could bandage a cut, pick up for a missed ride, call a teacher, talk to a parent. Whatever it was, I could make it better. Not this time. This one was too big for Mom and it is why I've handed it over to God. We all get something sometimes in life that's just too big. It doesn't have to be huge, just too big for you, and God will take it as long as you ask. It is such a comforting feeling to know we can do that. This one is definitely in His mighty hands and I, too, rest in His palm. When and where He lays us down may not be the green pasture we anticipated. Instead He may choose to place us in a dry field to farm. Either way, it's up to God and we have to trust Him.

I wish you enough
Peace and Love,
Sue

No matter how big our situation is, we have the choice to reside in a place of hope or hopelessness. We can fold or follow. Not only is it not in my character to fold, but as a Christian, I am strengthened by God's word and encouraged to follow with certainty. I often wonder why anyone would choose hopelessness. If you found yourself lost on a rugged trail, exhausted, out of water and someone shows up and tells you that he knows the way, would you sit down and die or stand up and follow? Jesus said "I am the way."(John 14:6) So when I get lost or tired or hungry or afraid or lonely, I choose hope and I follow Christ "Who strengthens me" **(Philippians 4:13)**.

2 Corinthians 1:4 "who comforts us in all our troubles
so that we can comfort those in any trouble
with the comfort we ourselves receive from God."

CHAPTER 9

Listening and Praise

Journal Entry
January 1, 2007

Well, a brand new year is stretched out before us to make of it whatever we wish. We have a choice! We can complain that 2006 was a disappointment or we can get excited about the possibilities that 2007 holds. We can let our thoughts and emotions be consumed with Robbie's condition and ask "Why?" every day, or we can know and feel God's hands at work and celebrate every moment that He shows us a reason even just for that day. Every time someone opens his or her heart or gives from somewhere deep or loves better or talks nicer or hugs longer or calls more often or speaks Jesus' name for the first time in a long time because of what has happened here, we can smile and we can know that God has not forgotten Robbie. No, He has not forgotten him at all. He has faith in Robbie to be exactly who he is being to all of us. Yea, it's going to be a good year.

I wish you enough
Peace and Love,
Sue

**1 Thessalonians 5:18 "Give thanks in all circumstances;
for this is the will of God in Christ Jesus for you."**

Journal Entry
October 15, 2006

I can remember way back in the beginning of our journey when morning came like a bully teasing us with another twelve hours of trail to endure. Now, when the sunlight comes through my own bedroom window and I hear the sound of birds instead of sirens, I invite the day to come. The coolest thing about faith is that when you have it, anything is possible and a new day is like a stage set for a potential miracle. The curtains open (clouds part). The lights go on (sun rises). The music sounds (birds) and the day (stage) is set for God to direct the performance. If He chooses rain, it rains. If He hollers "Bring in the storm!" it storms. And if He points to Robbie and says "center stage for a miracle," then it is so. Faith is believing that it can happen, and that is the easy part of faith. The difficult part is holding onto it if it doesn't happen. God says "no" sometimes just like Mom said no to the party you wanted to go to, or Dad said no to the guy you wanted to date. We all have to believe that "no" is sometimes the right answer and the only answer that brings us to where we are supposed to be in life. At the same time, I see in my mind Robbie standing tall before me once again and somewhere in my gut, I still believe that God will allow it. I intend to keep asking and continue to reside in a place of hope.

I wish you enough
Peace and Love,
Sue

Matthew 7:7 "Ask and it will be given to you,
seek and you will find, knock and the door will be opened to you."

Mark 11:24 "Therefore I tell you, whatever you ask for in prayer,
believe that you have received it and it will be yours.

Philippians 4:6 Do not be anxious about anything,
but in every situation, by prayer and petition, with thanksgiving,
present your requests to God. "

In a place of hope, the word "no" does not exist. I like to believe it is replaced with the word "wait." "Wait" is not as difficult because it reassures us that God is working. One very valuable thing that waiting provides is an opportunity to listen. Listening for God's voice is something that takes practice. It takes a certain level of dedication and it definitely requires a relationship. Since Robbie's injury, I feel that my listening skills have improved. I cannot believe that God has forgotten me, so the only other thing to believe is that He is beside me. The knowledge of His presence makes me want to hear His voice and feel His breath on my cheek. And so I listen. A word of encouragement, a feeling of contentment, an affirmation or simply an "I love you" will come to me in the most profound way, a way that tells me it can only be my Father's voice.

Journal Entry
November 3, 2006

I had a pretty cool thing happen to me today. I was returning home from taking my daughter to my brother's house. I was listening to a song a friend had given me on a CD and told me I should hear it. It's called "Praise You in This Storm." As it was playing, I was witnessing a breathtaking sunset over the bay. The words of the song struck me "I was sure by now that you would have reached down and wiped our tears away, stepped in and saved the day, but once again, I say 'Amen' and it's still raining. And as the thunder rolls, I barely hear you whisper through the rain, 'I'm with you.' And as your mercy falls, I raise my hands and praise the God who gives and takes away." Then the chorus "I'll praise you in this storm, and I will lift my hands, for you are who you are, no matter where I am, and every tear I've cried you hold in your hand. You never left my side and though my heart is torn, I will praise you in this storm." As the sun sank, so did my heart as the song broke it into pieces, but somehow

I grew strong and began to pray. I gave God my "bring it on" attitude and I said, "Lord, I am available to be used by you!" I continued, "Guide me Father in what I say and do and let my words and actions be a witness to others that you live in me!" I was getting louder, "My prayer is that you will use me for your glory!" It was like I wasn't afraid anymore and I really meant to tell Him that I'm okay and that I can do this and that He can use me. Then, with a little impatience and much passion in my voice, I shouted with all I had in me, "God! In the name of Jesus Christ your Son, my Lord and Savior ... heal my son!" At this very moment, the sun had sunk into the bay, and the song was rising with a loud ending of instrumental and the words, "I praise you in this storm." My emotions were running high and suddenly the song came bellowing out of the front left speaker of my car with the words: "Every tear I've cried, you hold in your hand. You never left my side." Well, NOTHING has come out of that front left speaker since it broke a year ago. I think that's cool. I think that's God. He said in **Psalm 91:15, "He will call on me and I will answer him."** *I called. He answered.*

I wish you enough
Peace and Love,
Sue

I believe that God wants us to call on Him! If we have a question, question Him! If we are afraid, tell Him! If we don't call on Him, how do we expect Him to calm our storm? In Mark 4: 35-40, Jesus' disciples found themselves in a boat with our Savior and as the waves rose and the wind kicked up, they grew afraid. They went to Jesus.

Mark 4:35-40 "That day when evening came, he said to his disciples, 'Let us go over to the other side'. Leaving the crowd behind, they took him along, just as he was, in the boat. There were also other boats with him. A furious squall came up, and the waves broke over the boat, so that it was nearly swamped. Jesus was in the stern, sleeping on a cushion. The disciples woke him and said to him, 'Teacher, don't you care if we drown?' He got up, rebuked the wind and said to the waves, 'Quiet! Be still!' Then the wind died down and it was completely calm. He said to his disciples, 'Why are you so afraid? Do you still have no faith?'"

Even though God has answered me and comforted me over and over again, I still have moments when I ask in a panic the question, "Do you not care if I drown?" And I hear Him asking me, "Why are you so afraid?" I can remember one specific night, after a week of little food and very little sleep, I was trying to comfort Robbie in his pain, ease his fear, wake him from nightmares, scratch his morphine itches, wipe his tears, and whisper in his ear how much I love him. I was doing everything I could, everything a mother is expected to do. I was packing him in ice to battle the nightly fevers and I realized just how big it all was. I could not keep the temperatures down. The fevers were winning and I was tiring. I felt the waves breaking over the boat and the wind ripping through my sails. Like his disciples in the boat, I was terrified. I thought, *Why is this happening? Where is my God? How can I do this on my own? We are going to drown*! Then, like His disciples, I went to Him. All I asked for was that He would hold us, that He would strengthen us, and that He would calm our storm. I was afraid. Three more nights and the fevers subsided. God will calm your storm, too, if you believe that He resides on the stern of your boat. Seek Him. Ask Him. If He can rebuke the wind and quiet the waves, He can certainly stop a fever, and He did. If what I receive in prayer brings me love, comfort, joy, contentment, peace, hope, or affirmation, then it can *only* come from God. One day He used a little boy to remind me that He is still with us on this journey.

Journal Entry
May 17, 2007

I worked at the restaurant tonight. It's a little Mexican place in Avalon called Tortilla Flats. I began working there when I was twenty-one years old and still enjoy serving people after twenty-three years. It was fairly busy and nice to be back waiting on and meeting people. A family of four came in after having been away all winter. The woman asked me how my winter was. I told her I had a good winter and was going to leave it at that, but as we talked, I ended up telling her that Robbie had been injured last summer and things were different. Her young son at the table interrupted, "Oh! Robbie Wunder! We pray for him at school every day!" I said, "Wow! That's cool! What school do you go to?" (thinking it was local) He named his school "St. Dennis in Havertown, PA." His mother said he was in fifth grade and his teacher's name was Lisa Hoban ... my cousin! And here on this night, I'm waitressing and Nicky Steller comes all the way to the shore, to my work, sits at my table and tells me that his class has been praying for my son almost a year now. That is so cool. Nicky was an angel.

I wish you enough
peace and love,
Sue

God used David to defeat Goliath **(1Sam 17).** He used Miriam to see Moses safely into the arms of the pharaoh's daughter **(Exodus 2).** He used Esther to save her people from being massacred **(Esther 7),** Moses to lead his people to the Promised Land **(Exodus 14),** and Nicky to remind me that He is still working and has not forsaken us.

CHAPTER 10

An Expanded View

T here are days when I forget to listen, when I'm tired or sad or simply wondering if I'm where I'm supposed to be in all this. It is on these days that I am filled with questions and yearning for answers. I used to drop the kids off at school and shoot down the road to the back bay where I could sit and be with God for a half hour before work. I would read a section of scripture or say a prayer or just sit in silence and listen. Well, on this particular day, all I could see before me was motion. The clouds were swiftly drifting across the sky. The water was choppy and the current carried it quickly as little waves splashed against the dock. Seagulls flew about and worked on broken clamshells, scavenging for a meal. I saw little fish breaking the surface of the water just enough to catch the early sun on their shiny scales. *Everything* was moving and I as I watched I began to cry and I asked him, "Why, Lord? Why is everything moving but my son? Why, when you created the breeze and the current and wings and fins and legs do you take away? Why have you taken away my son's ability to move like the world around him?" I searched the sky for an answer, the water for a clue, but there was nothing and so I wiped my eyes, started my car, drove off without an answer.

The next morning was cold and cloudy, and still. I dropped the kids off at school and, like an obedient child, I went to my spot at the bay to be with Him. Today, I saw a different picture. The clouds were low and heavy and they hung motionless from what appeared to be just feet above the surface of the water. The bay was frozen and nothing broke or skimmed the surface. There was no sign of birds or fish or wind or life. Suddenly, there in front of me was the answer to the question I asked the morning before. "Your vision is limited. Trust me." I realized that above the heavy dark clouds were birds flying and a sun dancing in the sky. Below the frozen water, there was the same current I watched the day before. Crabs crawled across the bay floor. There were fish and plants and activity that I couldn't see. The day before, I had a wider lens that included an endless blue sky, bouncing waves glistening in the sun, and splashes of life on the water's surface. But suddenly on this morning I was only seeing a sliver of what was. As I looked at the space between the clouds and the frozen surface, I realized it did not show the life, the movement, the whole picture. And so it reminded me to trust, once again, to remember God's box lid and how wonderful the entire masterpiece must be. He said, "Trust me, there is more to it than you can see." I cannot help but think of the story of Abraham and Isaac.

Genesis 22:1-14 "Some time later,

God tested Abraham. He said to him, 'Abraham!'

'Here I am.' he replied. Then God said, 'Take your son, your only son,

Isaac, whom you love, and go to the region on Moriah. Sacrifice him

there as a burnt offering on one of the mountains I will tell you about.'

Early the next morning Abraham got up and saddled his donkey. He

took with him two of his servants and his son Isaac. When he had cut

enough wood for the burnt offering, he set out for the place God had

told him about. On the third day, Abraham looked up and saw the

place in the distance. He said to his servants, 'Stay here with the

donkey while I and the boy go over there. We will worship and then

we will come back to you.' Abraham took the wood for the burnt

offering and placed it on his son Isaac, and he himself carried the fire

and the knife. As the two of them went on together, Isaac spoke up

and said to his father Abraham, 'Father?' 'Yes my son?' Abraham

replied. 'The fire and wood are here,' said Isaac, 'but where is the

lamb for the burnt offering?' Abraham answered, 'God himself will

provide the lamb for the burnt offering, my son.' And the two of them

went on together. When they reached the place God had told him

about, Abraham built an altar there and arranged the wood on it. He

bound his son, Isaac, and laid him on the altar, on top of the wood.

Then he reached out his hand and took the knife to slay his son. But

the angel of the Lord called out to him from heaven. 'Abraham!

Abraham!' 'Here I am,' he replied. 'Do not lay a hand on the boy,' he

said. 'Do not do anything to him. Now I know that you fear God, because you have not withheld from me your son, your only son.' Abraham looked up, and there in a thicket he saw a ram caught by its horns. He went over and took the ram and sacrificed it as a burnt offering instead of his son. So Abraham called that place, 'The Lord Will Provide'."

Talk about only seeing part of the picture and trusting! Abraham had no idea that while he traveled up one side of a mountain with his son, the Lord was sending a ram up the other side He did not know the details, but he knew his God. He knew his God would provide and so he proceeded in faith.

Hebrews 11:1 "Now faith is confidence in what we hope for and assurance about what we do not see."

We all ask God for explanations, but we do not listen close enough for the answer, because we are listening for a specific answer. We are waiting for the "answer to our prayers." What we need to do is open our eyes and our hearts and take what comes, knowing it is what should be, not necessarily what we *thought* should be. Remember, we do not know what is best. He does. God places each of us exactly and ever so carefully where we are, and it is His will—not ours—that matters. Through all of this, I have felt His presence and so I go on down this path unafraid and confident that He is leading us somewhere good. He said to the prophet in **Habakkuk 1:5 "I am going to do something in your days that you would not believe even if you were told."** No matter what we go through and how much sweat is on our brow at the end, the path, when followed in faith, with trust, always leads back to Him. Sometimes, a simple reminder of His presence is all we need.

Journal Entry
March 11, 2007

We got home from therapy today and I needed to lie down. I had hit the wall and went upstairs to try to catch an hour nap, when Hailey asked if I would take her and her friend for a walk on the beach. "Hail, I'm so tired and I don't feel well, not today." She left the room without argument and I immediately realized I was wrong. She needed me and so we went. When we arrived at the beach, she and her friend were off taking pictures and I walked alone. As I did, I began a conversation with God. I said to Him, "I'm tired today, but I've not given up." I said, "God, I have glorified your name in every celebration. I have praised you in the midst of this storm and no matter how battered my ship gets or how shredded my sails become, my anchor will continue to hold. I have been faithful to you, Lord. Please send me affirmation that we are on the right path and that you know my heart and how it breaks, and that Robbie will be okay. Send me something that I will know. Please. I'm listening. I'm looking. I need your hand now." I became very emotional and even demanding as I continued down the beach. I searched the water, the shells, found a few feathers, a stone, but nothing special until there lay His answer in the soft white sand at my feet. There lay a single section of a spine ... one vertebra. I knew immediately that it was Him. I put it in my pocket, said thanks, and when I left the beach, He was holding my hand.

I wish you enough
Peace and Love,
Sue

Isaiah 7:11 "Ask the Lord your God for a sign,
whether in the deepest depths or in the highest heights."

Listening is an active part in our relationship with God. You may see the vertebra in the sand as just a vertebra in the sand, but I choose to believe there is much more to this life and that God wants us to know it. If we use our listening skills, He leads us, shows us, and answers us. I believe that a better, more powerful place awaits us. I believe that God revealed this place to John while he was on the island of Patmos. John describes heaven with walls made of jasper, a foundation of precious stones such as topaz, ruby, and emeralds, and a wide city street "of gold as pure as transparent glass." I was watching a game show on television called *The American Bible Challenge* and a question was, "What percentage of Christians believe that the street in Heaven is literally paved with gold?" The answer was around 70 percent. It is said that God revealed the information to John and he documented it for us to know. So why do the other 30 percent of Christians not believe it? It is too farfetched? I do not think so! The planet we live on now, the world that God created and placed us in, contains all these precious stones and metals! Why would Heaven not be abundant in those things that are rare and precious to us? I laugh because a road paved in gold seems like a small feat. I cannot wait to see the big stuff! Knowing that the Lord has prepared a place for us is why we need to focus while we are here. No, this is not all there is, my friend, but it is all we have to prepare ourselves for Him, and that makes it precious. Our life here presents opportunities to move toward God or away from God every day. It is during our stay on earth that we are given constant choices to follow or stray, to believe or doubt, to care or not care, to remember or forget. As we travel from birth to death in this human vehicle, we become someone through the interpretation of our experiences, and hopefully on the day we are called, we are proud to introduce that someone to Jesus. We are sent down paths that are poorly lit simply to see if we reach for the light. Whether we reach for it or stumble blindly has a tremendous impact on the ease with which we travel, as well as our final destination. The day Robbie was injured, I reached for the light and since then, I've not stumbled. I've had many opportunities to question, doubt, forget, or just sit in the dark and cry, and believe me I *have*, but I move on because something comforts me, and this comfort that I feel can only be Him. I am becoming someone through my experience. I have definitely become more aware of my surroundings and the feelings that arise in me because of what happens in front of me, around me, and within me. Robbie's injury changed the color, the brightness, and sharpness of everything I look at. It changed not only the meaning of everything that happens, but the value of it and the purpose of each event. Perhaps because I needed better vision to make sense of his situation, its improvement brought everything into focus for me. I want to understand. I want to learn. I want to grow. Because of my sharpened sight, I learned a beautiful lesson on gratitude one morning from an old teacher on a bike. Years ago, he would have been a passerby, a dot on my life's canvas—even a blurry smudge, if you will. But on this particular day, he was a lesson.

Journal Entry
February 9, 2007

I was driving down the road on my way to work this morning and I saw an old man on a bike. It was bitter cold and although he wore a warm hat and coat, I couldn't help but notice he had no gloves. His basket was filled with what looked like junk, but it was probably valuable to him. His hair was rather long and hung out the back of his wool cap. As he went by, I wondered if he had a home, if he had eaten breakfast, and if his hand were terribly cold on the metal handlebars. A passing thought. Then I stopped at the store and, on my way in, I noticed his bike leaning against the building. I was curious and went in to look for him. I was drawn to him for some reason and I wondered about him. There he was at the counter purchasing a pair of gloves. The woman at the counter asked if he wanted a bag or if he was going to wear them. He motioned that he would wear them, but he didn't speak. I followed him out the door and as he headed for his bike, I headed for my car that I had kept running to stay warm. I sat there a minute wondering why I happened upon this man on this morning. I looked at him a moment and noticed him struggling with that little piece that the factories use to attach the right glove to the left. I climbed back out of my car and asked him, "Can I give you a hand with that?" He looked at me and handed over the gloves. I removed my gloves and very easily separated the hooks with my warm, young, able fingers. When I handed the gloves back to him, he looked at me with the most beautiful blue eyes, and his quiet lips motioned the words, "Thank You," followed by a warm smile. I felt good that I was able to help and I felt proud that I recognized someone needing it and I was glad that God put me in this man's path to perform a simple favor. But as I write this, I realize what really happened. This man was placed in my path to see if I would notice what he stood for. He reminded me of the simple things I take for granted, like warmth and youth and strong hands and a voice to say, "Thank you." I wasn't the hero after all. He was. He was the gift. So I try to remember him often and to share my warmth, to value my health, to use my hands to give and to let my voice be heard. If we listen closely, we are spoken to in these subtle but wonderful ways. And when we hear, we learn and we grow.

    If we simply follow Jesus' command in **John 13:34** to "**love one another**," we in return are gifted with love and lessons. I have shared scripture with you so far that tells us to "love one another," "carry each other's burdens," "give and it will be given to you," "be generous to the poor," "remember those in prison," "be open handed and freely lend whatever is needed," "be humble, gentle, patient, bearing with one another," and "wash one another's feet." It is really quite simple ... be nice. This reminds me of an opportunity I had to present my twelve-year-old daughter Hailey with a lesson on compassion. Sometimes, being nice is difficult when life is weighing us down. That is where compassion comes in. We stopped at a deli for snacks one afternoon. I waited in the car while Hailey and her girlfriend went inside. There was a woman working alone. Hailey and her friend could not decide what to get and the woman was obviously impatient and bothered. Finally, the girls bought what they wanted and left the store. Hailey got into the car and said, "Jeeze! That lady was nasty! She hollered at us and told us to make up our minds. I did not like her at all!" I said, "Honey, it is late in the afternoon and that lady has worked a double shift today. You see, her little girl is in the hospital and as soon as she gets off tonight, she is going right to the hospital to sit by her baby's bed until morning." I said, "Don't be mad at her. She's just tired and worried about her little girl." Hailey's demeanor softened and she looked at me and said, "Aw, that's a shame. How do you know that? Do you know them?" I smiled and said, "No, I don't know if that's true, but what if it was?" Hailey said, "If it was, I'd feel bad for her." So I said, "Then for whatever reason that lady was miserable, feel bad for her anyway and say a prayer for her instead of being angry with her." It was a good lesson for Hailey and for me. In teaching our children, we remind ourselves how love should work.

1 Peter 3:8 "Finally, all of you, be like-minded, be sympathetic, love one another, be compassionate and humble."

Ephesians 4:32 "Be kind and compassionate to one another, forgiving each other, just as in Christ God forgave you."

Journal Entry
December 19, 2006

We visited Robbie's fifth grade teacher, Ms. Fiore, and her class today. They had sent letters to Robbie months ago, and we wanted to respond. I was so proud of Robbie. He positioned himself in front of the class and answered questions for almost 45 minutes. The kids were so intrigued to have a person with a disability right there to answer their questions. They wanted to know what it felt like to be paralyzed, what school was like in a wheelchair, what his chair could actually do, how he types and eats and *gets into his bed, and someone even asked how he goes to the bathroom. Robbie sat and listened and answered every question. Afterward, his teacher informed us that one of her students handed in an odd amount of money during a fundraiser they did for Robbie. His name was Ryan M. and he donated thirty-six dollars and fifty cents. When asked about it, he said it was his money and his mom told him he could give it to Robbie. Robbie asked to see Ryan in the hallway. There he stood, almost eye-to-eye with Robbie. "Hey, what's up, man?" Robbie said. "Nothing," Ryan shrugged and put his hands in his pockets. "Yo, thanks for all that money you gave me. That's pretty awesome. Were you saving up for something?" Robbie asked him. "Well, yea, I was going to get a new skateboard when I had enough, but I don't really need a skateboard," he said. "Wow! And you gave it to me. That's really cool, man! Thanks a lot, Ryan," Robbie said. I told Ryan that if Robbie can get surgery to help him walk again someday, we would use his $36.50 towards it, and we let him know how much we appreciated his gift of kindness. He smiled and shrugged again as he said, "Okay," and went back to class. As I watched Robbie interacting with these children, I knew that God was using Robbie to do something great.*

I wish you enough
Peace and Love,
Sue

Some days are easier than others. Some days it all makes sense and other days it is confusing and painful. We have to expect a balance I suppose of pain and joy. How else do we recognize light if we have no darkness in which to shine it?

Journal Entry

January 9, 2007

For some reason, there were several weak moments for me today, but a good day in all because I'm still standing. I felt like I was being mocked all day by the circumstances. The first stone came whirling at me as I parked my car at the school. The groundskeeper saw the racks on my truck and asked me, "Do you surf?" "Nahh, my son does." The words pierced the morning peace, and our conversation continued like the turning of a steel blade already embedded in my chest. "I have a beautiful old nine-foot Ron Jon board I'm trying to sell if you're interested," he said. "Ahhh, no thanks," I replied, "he's got a great board." and I said goodbye with a smile, but it hurt. As the morning wore on, I got over it and I even started thinking about Robbie on a modified board and the possibilities. Then another stone struck me square in the face in the form of dangling car keys. A student of mine had just gotten his license and he was so excited. Dangling the keys in front of my face, he said, "It feels so good to drive!" Robbie couldn't wait to drive. He had had his permit and was due to get his license three months after he was injured. Anyway, the fact that things are different taunted me all day and teased me that nothing would ever be the same for Robbie. Then I wondered why I was letting it get to me. Things don't have to be the same. They can change and be different and it can be okay. So much is impossible for us, but ALL things are possible through Christ. We don't have to suffer the impact of a stone, but can catch it in our hand, grind it into powder, and pave a new road. It is our choice. Yea, my son will surf and he will drive if he wants to. I'm not going to cry because things are not the same. Thank God, things are still possible. Today, your life might change and become different. If God changes your direction, be not afraid but grateful, for He knows you best. It is what I've learned. I am glad my eyes were opened to that today.

I wish you enough
Peace and Love,
Sue

1 Timothy 4:4 "For everything God created is good, and nothing is to be rejected if it is received with Thanksgiving."

I do not think those weak moments will ever cease as long as I am traveling in a human body. My desire however, is to have more Christ and less me involved in all my ways. The comfort that I feel in trying moments is in the knowledge that the Holy Spirit resides in me. In the book of John, chapter 14, Jesus tells His disciples that He would be going away, but that

He would actually always be with us. He said in verse 16: **"And I will ask the Father and he will give you another counselor to be with you forever—the Spirit of truth. The world cannot accept him because it neither sees him nor knows him. But you know him for he lives with you and will be in you."** Later in verse 26, Jesus says, **"But the Counselor, the Holy Spirit, whom the Father will send in my name will teach you all things and remind you of everything I have said to you. Peace I leave with you; My peace I give you. I do not give as the world gives. Do not let your hearts be troubled and do not be afraid.** And, finally, in chapter 16, verse 33, He says, **"In this world you will have trouble. But take heart! I have overcome the world."** So when we find ourselves confused, in pain, troubled and afraid, we need to remember what Jesus said and know that we are not alone. There is a Holy Spirit within us that comforts, teaches, reminds, and protects. God put it there and it was that spirit that changed my thoughts that day and strengthened me.

1 Corinthians 3:16 "Don't you know that you yourselves are God's temple and that God's Spirit lives in you?"

CHAPTER 11

How Can He Love Me?

Sometimes it is difficult to believe that Jesus did what He did for us, that He died for our sins that we should have eternal life. He was mocked, flogged, nailed to a cross and left to die so that we may reside with Him in eternity, that our bare feet should tread upon a golden road, and that our sorry sinful souls should be held in God's forgiving arms. We have done nothing to deserve this. It is by God's grace that we are saved. That kind of love is incomprehensible. I was watching a video on Youtube called "The Awe Factor" that shows God's amazing creation and how we fit into it, and although the video was supposed to awe me, I found myself in a place of doubt because of just how big God is and how small I am. The video begins with a shot of a mountain and as the camera moves away, you see the curvature of the earth. Then, from 100,000 kilometers away, you see the earth. The camera moves to 1,000,000 kilometers away and you see the moon and the earth in space. From 10 trillion kilometers, you see past the sun and all the planets. Then the camera shows only sun and stars from 10,000,000,000,000,000 kilometers away. From 10 light years away you can only the see the sun and about eleven neighboring stars. Then from 1,000 light years away, it shows just a cluster within the Milky Way galaxy and in that Milky Way galaxy, we are a spec. Then it draws back further and shows our galaxy within galaxies! And from 10 million light years away, we see several hundred galaxies but there's more! From 100 million light years away, the view is clusters of galaxies and ours isn't even visible because it is such a tiny speck in creation. I was awed by the video, but I was also frightened. As the camera moved away, I began to feel so small. I couldn't even imagine being noticed from the moon, let alone from millions of light years away. I looked at it and thought "How can a God possibly know me all the way down here, buried on a planet in a galaxy among several hundred galaxies? There's no way! I'm too small. I must be insignificant, simply a minute part of this massive organism. How can God know me and love me? *I'm just too small*, I thought. These thoughts scared me because I have known God's love. I have felt Him, have heard Him, have had a relationship with Him for years. He has comforted me, taught me, protected me, reassured me, and as faithful as He had been to me, I suddenly found myself wondering how it can possibly be. I began to pray. I began to thank God for everything in my life and I apologized to Him for my questioning and my doubt. I begged Him to somehow explain it to me. I think it is important that we not be afraid in moments of doubt and to be conscious of it so that when it creeps in, we know to run to Him. I ran to Him now, just like I did the night Robbie was injured. I asked Him to show me that I am not too small for His love. Well, it just so happened that that particular year, my teaching assignment was changed from teaching students with Down's syndrome life skills to high school language arts and biology. Now, I had never taught biology before, but in my attempt to teach the students about life science, I had them looking at the parts of a flower under a microscope just days after my prayer for an explanation. And it was then, as I looked at the stamen of a flower, that God answered me. I love gardening and flowers. I look forward to every spring when my gardens come to life, and I cannot wait to plant new flowers in all my pots, take photos of flowers, and share plants with friends. I love it! It is one of my simple joys in life. And as I looked at this tiny part from way inside the flower, I wondered … if this stamen had a mind, would it say, "There's no way she can love me. I'm too small and insignificant. What joy could I possibly bring her from way down here in the center of this flower among flowers, buried in her huge garden among gardens all over the earth?" A stamen is the reproductive part of the flower. It is the part that gives me more flowers! It is amazing and significant when it comes to my joy. And God said to me at that moment, "You are amazing and significant when it comes to my joy. I love you." I should have known that. I have His word.…

**Luke 12:6-7 "Are not five sparrows sold for two pennies?
Yet not one of them is forgotten by God.
Indeed, the very hairs of your head are all numbered.
Don't be afraid; you are worth more than many sparrows."**

Proverbs 8:17 "I love those who love me,
And those who seek me find me."

Knowing God loves me and knowing that He left in me His Holy Spirit to guide and counsel me is comforting, but it does not mean that life is always easy. It does not mean that moments are not going to break me down or tear me apart. It does not mean I am not going to doubt or stray or forget because I will and I do. Like I mentioned earlier, rather than ask Him not to send me, I ask Him to go with me. When I cry, I simply ask Him to wipe my tears. Knowing that He will makes them sting a lot less.

Journal Entry
June 19, 2007

This evening, I took Hailey into Stone Harbor to meet a friend, and after I dropped her off, I decided to go to the beach just for a minute, to take a deep breath of air and to see the ocean. Well, I saw the ocean, the same one everyone else was looking at. But it wasn't all I saw. I saw Robbie out there on the waves as clear as day. He was straddling his long board, looking out over his left shoulder, waiting for a ride to roll in. He wore a black, white, and red rash guard and a black bathing suit with red threading. His hair was long, streaked by the sun, and in his eyes of course. His nose was peeling, as it did from Memorial Day to Labor Day. Finally, a wave came as I stood there watching in my mind. He lay down, paddled hard, dropped in, and popped up. There he stood, 6'3" against a beautiful blue backdrop of a summer sky. I stood there staring at what seemed like an empty sea to the other people on the beach, but I was watching Robbie as I cried. If you have a chance today, take a mental picture of your child doing something that he or she loves and watch them like you may never see it again. Suddenly, it becomes precious, and what we may not have recognized as a gift when it was happening is now something we will always cherish. So cherish it and praise God for it without it having to be taken away to be appreciated. Thank God for every moment and praise Him for the gift of that moment.

I wish you enough
Peace and Love,
Sue

1 Chronicles 16:34 "Give thanks to the Lord, for He is good;
His love endures forever."

As time passes, we all leave things behind. We all change and proceed to new adventures, new interests, and new dreams. Whether we are forced to or choose to, we all move on. I may never see Robbie on a surfboard again, or on a four-wheeler or even driving a car, but I know because God has plans for him, I will watch him fly someday. Just because my plans for Robbie always involved an able body and independence does not mean that God's plans do. How many of us have "plans" for our children. We have ideas and dreams and expectations for them. Although it is wonderful to dream, do not forget the writer of the script is our mighty God, and His pen is so much more talented than ours. I am not going to stop dreaming. Because of my God, I am going to dream even bigger!

Journal Entry
July 15, 2007

I'm so glad Rob and I are able to be home in the summer. Rob works a few hours a day in his picture framing shop in our garage and I waitress a few nights a week, but mostly our days are free, and that is such a blessing, especially with two teenagers. So many kids are on their own these days. I'm just glad I've always been able to enjoy summer time with mine. As I look back at all the camping trips we took to Maine, Vermont, Massachusetts, Georgia, and North Carolina, I have so many good memories. A lot was taken from Robbie at sixteen years old, but when I think about his life up until then, I'm glad he got to do things he did while he was able-bodied. He's gone horseback riding in the mountains and white water rafting. He's been scuba diving in the Atlantic with sharks and snorkeling off the coast of the island of St. Thomas. He's been quad riding in upstate Pennsylvania. He's stood under water falls, swam in rivers, camped in the mountains, and enjoyed bonfires on the beach. He's been on a Caribbean Cruise and spent a month in England. He spent summers on the waves and even got to ski a few winters. He knows what it feels like to enjoy life. I don't want him to forget it. I want him to continue to feel the rush of life, because that passion does not reside in our bodies, but in our spirits. I hope his spirit continues to seek new things that make him feel just like he did when he was on a wave. I believe it will as soon as he realizes he can still fly.

I wish you enough
Peace and Love
Sue,

I had an opportunity to see that spirit in a group of young men at the rehabilitation hospital. When you wonder what it is that carries a person, motivates a person, inspires a person, and drives a person, you realize it is something more than just a person. It is a spirit. It is in us, and just as one's hearing may grow sharper if sight were taken away, I watched the spirit of these boys come alive as their bodies were silenced. After witnessing this scene, I could never deny the fact that there is so much more to us than a human body. I watched the "counselor" that Jesus spoke of, at work. He lifted, guided, strengthened, and protected these boys through a simple section of rough terrain on their journey toward a new life—a life that God knows will be different from anything they had in mind.

Sue Wunder

Journal Entry
August 30, 2006

Robbie's therapy session involved five teenage boys ages thirteen to nineteen, all injured that summer, sitting in a circle tapping a balloon around trying to keep in in the air. When the balloon drifted softly toward one of the boys, he would grit his teeth, lift an arm as if he were lifting a car, and as he swung with all his might, a gentle tap would send the balloon but a few inches into the air. Then he would smile. In this group was a hockey player, a soccer player, a dirt bike racer, a basketball player, and a surfer. During the activity, I could see the basketball player rebounding, the soccer player head-butting, the hockey player shifting his weight from side to side down the ice, the dirt bike rider pulling up hard on the handlebars over a jump, and I saw Robbie on a wave taking it all the way in. I realized that although each of these guys is leaving their passion as they know it, behind, they still have it in them. I saw it. And I realized that it is not what we do that makes us who we are, but what we carry within us. And it was comforting to see that these boys were still carrying all the good stuff that went off the playing field on a stretcher, with them. They were still them! I pray that each one realizes that when they leave this hospital, even if it is with a lot less than what they hoped for physically, they are still going to have everything that matters to live a good life because, after all, it's not what we do with our hands that makes a life good. It is what we do with our hearts and everything it took to tap that balloon today came from way down deeper than a muscle. I hope each of these boys know what their hearts are capable of in this life.

I wish you enough
Peace and Love,
Sue

CHAPTER 12

Salvaging After Loss

When we suffer loss—whether it is an ability, a loved one, a job, a possession, whatever it is—there comes a time when we have to gather up what we have left and continue down life's path. After a storm, we rummage through the wreckage. We collect every possible thing we deem valuable and we take it with us. Sometimes it is tiny, but it is all we need to propel us forward. After hurricane Sandy devastated the east coast in 2013, there were endless news clips and stories of personal loss. One story in particular comes to mind when I think about the process of salvaging after loss. Superstorm Sandy sparked a blaze that engulfed over eighty homes in Breezy Point, Queens, New York. There was a news clip of a grey-haired woman salvaging through the charred remains of her neighborhood. All she could find was a small piece of a blue and yellow plate from what used to be her kitchen. She picked it up and, with tears rolling down her face, she brushed it off, put it in her pocket, and took it with her. That tiny piece of a plate was all she had, but the value of it is something no one but she could comprehend. Perhaps that fragment of blue and yellow clay will take her back to a Sunday dinner with her family or the wedding day she received the set of yellow and blue dishes, or a plate of cookies surrounded by the neighborhood children.

Perhaps one of her own children or grandchildren painted the plate on a rainy afternoon at Grandmom's house. No matter what, it was what was left and she picked it up and took it with her. She lost her home and all of her possessions, but she salvaged the memories and the love. And that yellow and blue piece of the past that she tucked into her pocket holds within it everything God let her keep. So when we lose, when devastation or tragedy strikes, remember to salvage. It is important to take something with us because it is that very thing that God allowed us to keep that will be the beginning of a new us. I have learned that God never takes it all. Think about it. What has He left you with, and what have you done with it? I know a lot has been taken away from Robbie, but I thank God He did not take it all. I was devastated the night the doctor told me that all Robbie had left physically was bicep muscles to bend his arms and the ability to lift his wrists. To me that was comparable to a fragment of one plate from a lifetime of possessions. But it was something. And I am amazed how that tiny something becomes everything. Because Robbie can bend his arms and lift his wrists, we can put a brace on his hand so he can feed himself, hold a drink, use a pen, type a paper, make a phone call, adjust his glasses, rub his nose, shake a hand (with a closed fist,) propel his wheelchair, wave goodbye (with a closed fist), and my favorite, give a hug. With two working muscles, I believe he will do so much. There is a saying that states something to the fact that it is not what you have that makes you special, but what you *do* with what you have that makes you amazing. I honestly believe that Robbie is already amazing, but what he does with what he has salvaged will be even more remarkable.

Journal Entry
November, 8, 2006

Robbie's favorite class since he entered high school has been architectural drawing. He has even considered going to college for architectural design. Last year, he was having difficulty with algebra and said to me, "I guess I will never be an architect if I stink at algebra." I told him he could do whatever he wanted and that if that's his dream, don't let anything stop him. Now, still wishing to be an architect, he not only needs to hurdle algebra, but the fact that there is a possibility he may never regain the use of his hands. Still, I tell him to chase it. I told him that if a person can perfect the skill of hitting a golf ball with a metal rod 300 yards into a tiny hole, then he can perfect drafting with paralyzed hands. Anyway, I came home from work today and he told me to go look on his bed. I went into his room alone and there on his bed was a beautiful, perfect, technical drawing of a "stepped shaft" with a grade of 100 percent on it. Not one mistake! I sat down on the bed and I cried, not because he did it, but because he chose to try and he believed he could and he succeeded! I came out of his room in tears, blabbing, "It's beautiful. It's perfect." He said as he rolled his eyes at my silly sentimentality, "Do you even know what a stepped shaft is?" I cried, "It doesn't matter what it is. You drew it and it's perfect." He smiled at my joy. I asked him how long it took and he said an hour to do what would normally take fifteen minutes. Then he said, "I'll get faster." At that moment, I thanked God for the biceps and the wrist extension that He let Robbie keep.

I wish you enough,
Peace and Love,
Sue

One thing I have learned in all of this is that what we have today may be lost tomorrow. Gifts are just that—gifts. They are to be accepted with gratitude and embraced. I remember being on the beach with my brothers and my sister. It was a quiet afternoon, not a whole lot going on. It was actually getting a little boring. We were considering packing up and going home, as it was getting late in the day. All of a sudden, out of nowhere appeared a gigantic beach ball! It was the biggest beach ball I had ever seen, and it came right at us. We all jumped up and began playing with this massive, colorful ball. We were passing it around, kicking it, batting it back and forth, chasing it in the wind. My brother Danny rolled up one side of it and down the other as we all laughed and clapped. We played like little children, as if this ball awakened our spirits. After about twenty minutes of fun and laughter, just as quickly as it appeared, it was swept out to sea. We stood there as it drifted out of reach, then watched it grow smaller and smaller as the waves tossed it about. Finally, it disappeared and we decided to leave the beach. As we walked off the beach, we recapped the experience and laughed together. When I think back on what happened there, I realize how precious a moment is and how important it is to recognize a gift when it lands on the shore of our lives. Whether it is fifteen minutes of laughter or fifteen years of love, it is to be cherished. It is to be embraced, enjoyed, shared, and appreciated. And if the wind should kick up and take it from you, do not collapse in the sand and cry for the loss, but walk off the beach celebrating the gift.

Journal Entry
October 11, 2006

I went to pick up Hailey from a school trip tonight and I got to the school at six. Her bus didn't show up until seven. It was a blessing because I opened the window of my car, put my head back, and closed my eyes. The silent, damp shore air drifted in and the smell of home that I had missed so much the past three months lulled me to sleep. The city was so noisy, but I didn't know loud until I heard peace. I think many of us live that way ... fast and noisy and busy. We don't know it until, if we are lucky, a quiet moment comes our way. I'm sure some parents were bothered that the bus was an hour late. I'm grateful. It turned out to be an opportunity to accept another gift—forty minutes from God, sweet peace.

**James 1:17 "Every good and perfect gift comes from above,
coming down from the Father of the heavenly lights,
who does not change like shifting shadows."**

Change is another thing we need to embrace. When it comes upon us suddenly, we rarely welcome it. Instead, we panic and try desperately to avoid it. As humans, we become comfortable in sameness, in repetition, in believing we know what the next moment holds. We become content with where we are, who we are with, what we do, and what we have. When Robbie was injured, the fact that "nothing will ever be the same" was frightening to Hailey. I wanted her to know that it did not have to be, and that change is okay. What many of us do not understand, especially in the midst of change, is that it is necessary.

Journal Entry
September 10, 2006

Today was a good day. Sometimes I only know that by the way I feel inside when I sit down at night. Funny thing is when I sit down to write, I have to think real hard about where yesterday ended and today began. It's a long road and the scenery here isn't changing. Fortunately, though, we are. Although the path and its obstacles remain constant, what happens within us is what makes the terrain easier to cover each day. That is what makes tomorrow new. Speaking of change, Hailey cried tonight because "nothing will ever be the same," and she's right. I got to thinking about that myself and I realized that the four people who left my house on the night of July 23 will be gathering again under the same roof in early October. Only, we are no longer the same four people. We have shared this experience as a family, yes, but it has also sent each of us on our own personal journey. Our makeup as a group will be different, but I believe we are all bringing home something good, something we didn't have before that will make life better. So, Hailey, you are right. It will never be the same, but because I know God's intentions are good, it will always be just fine.

I wish you enough

Love,

Sue

When you have faith that God is the author of your story, the artist of your portrait, and the director of your show, you can step into the script and let it take you on whatever journey He created with you in mind. Sometimes transitions are smooth and sometimes a chapter comes with an unexpected twist. When one of those twists, or changes spring up on a page in your story, and you find yourself in a place where you do not want to be, do not panic. Do not run from what appears to be darkness, but bring your light into it. Come at that change with everything you have. The same year Robbie was injured, my school district was going through some changes. Teachers were being reassigned. Jobs were being eliminated, and salaries were being cut. For some it was very difficult. I approached the staff and I gave them my new perspective, for I had learned against my will how to move with change.

Journal Entry
June 15, 2007

Dear Staff,

*I did not lose my job, so I do not know what **that** feels like. But because of what has just happened in my life, I know the fear of the unknown, the disappointment of loss, the anger of being struck, the anxiety of an unpredictable future, the testing of faith, and the panic of change. So I can tell you this: In September, when you walk into your new classroom or office, or you are still in bed because you haven't found a new job yet and deep in your gut you have this sick feeling because it is not where you want to be, I want you to think of something for me. I want you to think of Robbie's room. When Robbie is not home and I walk into his room, I have that feeling in my gut, that sick feeling when I look at the wheelchair, the lift, the shower chair, the monitor, the medical supplies, the typing aide, the ball mouse ... I hate it! It is not where I* *want to be. It is not where Robbie wants to be. But when he comes home, he fills that room with so much light and laughter that I don't even see those other things. I see him. I see his favorite art pieces, his hat collection, his sneaker collection, his movies, his friends, his drawings on the computer screen, his camera, and his books. I hear his laughter and his music. He makes that room different! He has taught me that we can do that wherever we are. It is our choice. We can go into a space and be sick about it and complain, or we can bring light into it and change it. Simply by accepting where he has been placed, by embracing what he has been left with, and by enjoying what surrounds him, Robbie has taken an enormous change, a tragic change and altered a script that would have been filed in the drama section, to one that finds itself among the inspirational stories with promising endings. We all have the ability to do that, and the choice is also ours.*

I wish you enough
peace and love,
Sue

The wonderful thing about change is that although things change around us and inside us, we hold on to unchanged memories, and oh, what a gift that is from our maker! Although many memories are painful, it is those that make us smile, laugh, feel gratitude, ignite our passion, or warm us that make the ability to remember, so precious. The fact that we have been gifted with the ability to collect in our minds, precious moments, makes life on earth meaningful. We can go back and choose the ones we want to carry forward. Even in the midst of painful recollection one day, I found joy.

Journal Entry
June 3, 2007

A friend from school stopped by today to retrieve some items for the day care she is opening upon retiring in June. As I went through the attic, the memories flooded my mind. I reluctantly handed over Robbie's little tikes easel, his cash register, and an "Easy Bake" oven that he and Hailey shared. I could still taste the warmed cookie dough and the mushy cake I had to scrape from the little tin pan. It may have been "cooked" by a light bulb, but it was prepared with pure love and determination, and hand delivered with pride. There was a "Light Bright" that I was about to give away and I couldn't. Not today. The image of Robbie's tiny fingers grasping those little plastic pegs and placing them in the pattern on the screen struck me. Little perfect working fingers ... I put the Light Bright back in the attic for now. What we save is amazing, isn't it? I don't mean in our attics. I mean in our hearts and minds. The human brain and body are phenomenal containers for what has been. The cool thing is that we can actually give away everything in the attic, but no one can take what we save in us. Memories, feelings, experiences are ours and this is true wealth. I'm going to give the Light Bright away now. I don't need it really. I have everything I need right here in my heart.

I wish you enough
Love,
Sue

CHAPTER 13

Choose To See Beauty

I find it interesting when nothing on the outside changes, but a change within us makes everything look different. I remember the first time we returned to the city after going home. As we came over the bridge, I felt good. My first days in the city were sad and frightening. The buildings surrounded me like brick walls forbidding me to escape. The sounds of life below the roof mocked me, as I felt imprisoned and paralyzed myself. The distance from home was cold and lonely. But this time, a certain warmth filled me as we drove into the lights and the life of the city. Now, it felt like a blanket that wrapped around my son and me and kept us for a time to heal. The sounds were not so mocking now, but familiar and kind like an old friend. The buildings felt like shelter now, not prison walls. It seems I have chosen to leave the pain somewhere below the subway and keep in my heart the good that came from my stay in the city. I learned. I grew. I became closer to people and met more. I experienced God's hand and I witnessed love like I never knew. I felt the rewards of generosity and selflessness. Now, when I go into the city, no pain lingers, only love.

Sue Wunder

**Psalm 30:5 "Weeping may stay for the night,
but rejoicing comes in the morning."**

Journal Entry
June 29, 2007

I went back to the beach this evening. I don't know why, but I wanted to go there again. It hurts so much but there's something there that I need. I am not sure what it is. Maybe I think I will find something that has been lost there. Maybe I want to watch the surfers and remember the part of my son I left on the waves. Yes, I want to remember, because I think going back is often part of moving on. We have to face pain and feel pain and understand what we are feeling before we can leave it and go ahead. I want to keep going to the beach until it stops hurting. I want to go there and not cry for what has been lost, but remember what once was and celebrate that every time my feet touch the soft white sand. I want to change the substance of my tears from the kind that sting my eyes to the kind that slide gently down my cheeks and rest on the corners of my upturned lips.

I wish you enough
Love,
Sue

Seven years later, I sat in that same spot on the beach. This time, Robbie sat under a pavilion 20 yards from the water reading a book. Did pain still linger? Of course. But gratitude and praise carry so much more power, and so I rested in that. I sat on the lap of my God and I praised him for every little gift I could possibly find in that moment. I thanked God again that he did not take my son from me. I thanked God that the temperature was just cool enough for Robbie to be out that day. I thanked God that Robbie *wanted* to return to the beach! I thanked God that Robbie was *healthy* enough to go to the beach. I thanked God that Robbie replaced his passion for surfing with a passion for reading, writing, film, and photography. I thanked God for the breeze, the blue sky, the quiet waves, the seagulls, and yea, even the surfers. By the time I was finished praising my God, I had little room in my heart for pain, sorrow, or complaints. Why would I even desire to find ugly, when God surrounds me with beauty? Satan is constantly trying to paint over God's work with his deceitful oils. Our protection against that is praise. In every moment, choose praise, choose gratitude, choose joy, choose God, and you will be lifted out of your dark place into light. I am convinced that choosing to worry or to give in to your pain takes more energy than to simply praise. Praising becomes a habit, and although it may take practice and a retraining of your way of thinking, once you have mastered the skill of seeing your surroundings lit with God's light, you will be happier and more content in your circumstances.

Journal Entry
June 3, 2007

I went for a run today in the pouring rain and it felt so good. The world gets quiet when it rains and everything intensifies in color and smell under God's sprinkler. As I was running, I felt like I knew a secret and that everyone who stayed inside today were missing out. In my first mile I stepped in a puddle and completely drenched my left foot. I laughed as my mind took me back to a wet Hildreth Road where we used to live. It was raining really hard. Robbie was about six years old and I suggested we go out and run in the rain, jump in a few puddles, and he was so into the idea. What six-year-old would not be into that? It was so much fun. Robbie still has the same giggle he had at age six, just a lot deeper. I'm so glad I still get to hear it. What a gift.

I wish you enough
peace and love,
Sue

A rainy day run is something I still do and it still feels like the best kept secret. It reminds me of my faith because no matter how awesome I tell people it is to run in the rain, they just do not get it. They see rain. They think cold and wet. But until you experience something, you just cannot imagine how awesome it is. My God is that way. People know what rain is and they are familiar with running and everyone has jumped in a puddle at some point in their lives, but it is the actual experience that brings forth all the feelings. People know about God. They have heard about Jesus and everyone has been to church at least once in their lives. But not everyone gets it because they have not experienced Jesus through an actual relationship. You cannot really know running in the rain unless you have run in the rain. Just the same, you cannot really know Christ unless you have actually had a relationship with Him, unless you have experienced Him in your life. I have to admit that the best relationships I have witnessed have been born out of trial and tribulation. Now I have mentioned that you do not need something bad to happen in your life to get close to God, but it certainly brings you to his feet in a rather timely manner if you are not already there. The purpose of sharing my journey on the pages of this book is to introduce you to my God and hope that my experiences motivate you to seek your own personal relationship with our Savior. And if I have convinced at least one reader to go for a run in the rain, well, that would make me happy, too.

CHAPTER 14

An Answer to My Prayer?

A s I write, I am sent back to my classroom where I taped to the window by my desk a prayer. I found the prayer printed on a yellow piece of card stock on a table in a church where I was taking Hailey for Girl Scout meetings. It was such a fitting prayer for the way I had been feeling at the time. I was frustrated that I was not doing enough and I asked God to use me in a greater capacity. I read the words on that yellow card every morning for two years, sometimes out loud, "Lord, I am available to be used by you every day. Guide me, Father, and lead me in what I say and do. May my words and actions be a witness to others that you live in me. To the lonely, may I be a friend. To those with heavy burdens, help me to meet their needs. Lord, I do not seek fame or fortune. My prayer is that you use me for your glory. I know I do not have much to offer, but what I have I give you. Guide me to be what you want me to be. More than anything else, may I be like your Son, my Lord and Savior. Amen!" As I continued my daily prayer, I researched possible mission trips that I could take in the summer, thinking that would be a way to serve and it would feel good to give of my time. I felt strong and confident that I could do whatever God needed me to do to glorify Him. I wanted to bring people's attention to my God and share with them what He is capable of.

It was during this time, while cleaning my attic, I came across a little pamphlet. It was titled, *The Purpose Driven Life*. I thought "perfect" and I excitedly tucked it into my pocket for later. I thought it might be just what I needed to give me some direction, a purpose, as was stated in the title. I read through the pamphlet later that night and it motivated me to go to church that Sunday (I hadn't been in a while). As I slipped into a pew, the priest began his sermon with a book in his hand. He held it up and asked, "How many of you have ever heard of this book, *The Purpose Driven Life*?" I was shocked! I had just found it the night before! Although mine looked different, smaller, it was the same title and author, so I was all ears. I was excited to hear what else the priest had to say. He talked about our purpose as Christians and God's purpose for us, our paths and our reason for having been created. He talked about knowing our gifts and using them.

This *coincidence* came and went. I mentioned to my husband how I had found the very book that was the topic of the day's sermon, but that was the extent of my sharing on the subject, until my birthday a few weeks later. I was having friends over to celebrate my birthday, and my friend Judy gave me the same book the priest had held up in church, *The Purpose Driven Life*! As if I had not already begun to believe that maybe I should pay attention to this book, two more friends gave it to me before my birthday week was over. I got the message. My running partner and dear friend Debby and I decided to read the book together and share our thoughts and insights. At the end of each chapter is a "Point to Ponder," which she and I agreed to put into writing and exchange. After each run, we would sit on the park bench and read each other's thoughts, then discuss in further detail where the chapter took us. It was a wonderful fellowship and I was beginning to feel moved toward the idea of serving on a deeper level. At this particular time in my life, I did not belong to a church, but was sporadically attending churches in the area. I would spend a Sunday at one church, then a few services at another church, a morning praying at the beach, a run in the woods, a Bible verse at the bay, but nothing consistent and eventually, nothing. We even stopped discussing the book as it began to talk about church fellowship, and neither of us had found a comfortable church setting, therefore failed to see the importance as we seemed to be growing just fine without one. (Little did I realize a church is not a building, but a group of people.)

Several weeks passed and I must say I became a rather complacent Christian. The desire was still in me, more or less simmering on the back burner, until the day a woman who taught in my district approached me on the playground while I was out with my students.

"You're Sue Wunder, aren't you?" she asked.

"Yes," I replied.

She continued, "This might sound very strange to you and I have never done this before, but I was in church last night and I received a very strong message. It was 'Tell Sue Wunder that her mother prays incessantly that she return to the Eucharist.'

I said "Wow!" but I was not surprised as I was aware of my mother's diligent prayer life, and no doubt her children would be the subject of most. I was very grateful that this woman had the courage to speak up. I called my mom that afternoon.

"Mom!" I told her the story and she replied "I do, dear. I pray every day that my children have God in their lives and Jesus in their hearts."

Then I asked about the Eucharist. "The woman used the word 'Eucharist.' She did not say 'return to God' or 'return to Christ' or 'return to church.' She said 'the Eucharist,' and for some reason, this tugs at me." We talked about it and Mom explained the importance of the Blessed Sacrament in the Catholic service as I had learned growing up. After our conversation, I figured it was time for me to go back to church. That Sunday, I once again slipped into a pew as the priest started his sermon. He said, "Today, I am going to talk about the Eucharist." I looked around like I was on candid camera. My eyes filled and my ears opened as I settled in to listen.

The Eucharist, also called Holy Communion, the Sacrament of the Altar, the Lord's Supper, and other names, is a Christian sacrament. It is reenacted in accordance with Jesus' instruction at the last supper, that His followers do in remembrance of Him as when He gave His disciples bread, saying, "This is my body," and gave them wine, saying, "This is my blood." The term "Eucharist," in Greek means "thanksgiving."

It all translated to me as an urgency for me to return to a place of remembrance and gratitude. I was to receive Jesus Christ, take Him in, digest His word, metabolize it and like it said in the prayer, "be a witness to others" that He lives in me. I was ready! I was pumped up and waiting for my assignment. I was thinking maybe find a way to reach the Autistic students in my class, or go overseas and feed the poor! Maybe I could do something great for mankind! Then I was stopped in my tracks.

I was at work and an annoying ache began in my neck. It did not hurt to move, but it was so intense I had to leave work not even an hour after it began. I went home and lay down. I got up to eat dinner, but after only ten minutes of being upright, the pain became unbearable and I went back to bed. By the middle of the night, I was banging on my chiropractor's door (my friend Debby) begging for help. She adjusted me and we called my family doctor for pain medication. Even after the medication, the pain continued to intensify. I ended up in the emergency room the next day, again to no avail. I went back to my bed and suffered. If I were to get up to simply use the bathroom, by the time I returned to my bed, I would be in tears from the pain. I lay there for six weeks. Debby came by and adjusted my spine on a daily basis. I grew very weak. I lost 18 lbs and my left arm atrophied because no signals were reaching it. Early on, I removed a very fine gold necklace with a cross on the end from my neck because of the pain, and I hung it on my doorknob. I remember reaching over and taking the cross in my hand and saying to God, "I know you have not forgotten me," and I waited as I slowly healed. My friend Leslie would stop by with fresh fruit salad every other day trying to get me to eat. Finally, I could stay upright for longer and longer periods of time and eventually the pain subsided. It was five weeks into my injury that I could actually handle going for an MRI and what it read amazes me now. The doctor said that my C5 vertebra was "indenting" my spinal cord. C5 is the same vertebra that Robbie shattered. I do not know if there is such a thing as a physical premonition, but I do know that when Robbie was injured weeks later, my body had just been through a forced cleansing and I had continued on a regime of fresh fruits, veggies, juicing, and prayer. In looking back, I feel as if my mind, body, and spirit had been prepared. I had also been humbled, reminded of my dependency on God and the fact that I am merely an instrument. My plans of doing something great for mankind as I patted myself on the back transformed into submitting myself to God's will. I still wanted to be used and waited for an answer to the prayer on the yellow card.

Years later as I stood before congregation after congregation giving my testimony, and now as I write this book, I wonder if this is not the assignment I asked for as I recited the words on my little yellow card. *Oh my God!* I thought, *had I made a mistake?* I agreed to serve yet, suddenly, I find myself pleading with God to let me take it back. "Wait a minute!" I holler. "I didn't say to use my *son*, my heart, and soul! I gave you a list of things, stipulations if you will, assignments I thought would be fun and inspirational. Ways *I* believed I could best serve. I wanted to pick the job!" Then I reel myself back in and collect what I know about my God and I realize that if we are truly open to serving our Lord, we do not get to say things like "I don't do windows." We offer ourselves completely and without restricting or modifying elements.

I have to believe there is something—a word, a phrase, a scripture, a moment, a story, a gift, something in this manuscript for at least one reader—that will give that split-second event that changed my life, that one inch difference between the deep and shallow end of a pool significance.

CHAPTER 15

What is Freedom?

A friend of mine's son, Matthew, was arrested shortly after Robbie was injured. He had been driving under the influence and a man lost his life. Matthew was sentenced to five-and-a-half years in prison. Although it was devastating, I remember thinking that it was only five-and-a-half years and he would be free again. I remember comparing it to Robbie's sentence of a lifetime in a wheelchair. I wished we were given a time, a date, a day when we could put it all behind us and move on. It didn't seem fair that Robbie's split-second mistake would never be paid off. Then I began to contemplate the word "freedom." What frees us from anything in life? People are imprisoned by brick walls and bars, wheelchairs and beds, yes, but what about guilt, regret, pain, abuse, debt, addiction, worry, greed, money, anxiety, and jealousy? I've come to realize that these are the true places of confinement. These things that take up residence in our being creep in while our faith sleeps and immobilize us. The issues that gnaw at us from within are far more benumbing than prison walls and wheelchairs. They are, in fact, lethal. Although our internal struggles can make us very ill, I am not referring to physical death, but instead to the deterioration and fatality of one's spirit. Recall a time when you suffered an assault from one of the things I mentioned above. Maybe a time when guilt swallowed you up or abuse knocked you to the ground. Maybe debt came tumbling down on you, or addiction wrapped itself around you so tight you couldn't breathe. Perhaps worry churned in your stomach or you caught an ugly glimpse of greed as you passed by a mirror. Has a hot pool of jealousy ever swallowed you up? How many precious moments in your lifetime have you wasted battling anxiety? So let me ask you this: Who are the disabled? Who are the imprisoned? And who of us are free?

When we accept Jesus Christ as our Savior, we are accepting the gift of the Holy Spirit He offers us in John 14. We are accepting the peace He gave us and the truth that He is the one and only Son of God who died for us. And this truth, Jesus says, will set us free. When Jesus offered the people freedom in John 8:32, they answered Him by saying that they were not slaves, so how could He free them? Obviously, Jesus was not referring to physical imprisonment when He replied in **John 8:34, "Very truly I tell you, everyone who sins is a slave to sin. Now a slave has no permanent place in the family, but a son belongs to it forever. So if the Son sets you free, you will be free indeed."** He was referring to spiritual bondage. The freedom He offers us is a light heart, a worry-free mind, and a faith-filled body that moves through life with His spirit inside navigating our every move, consuming our every thought, and leading us to the wonderful place He has prepared for us. Believe it not, you can get there through prison walls and by way of a wheelchair. Jesus did not die for our bodies, but for our souls. If guilt is your prison,

Jesus says, **"I will forgive ... "** (Heb 8:12). If it is worry, He says, **"Don't worry. Be hopeful"** (Matt 6:25). About easing your pain, He says, **"I am willing ... "** (Matt 8:2). About greed, He says, **"Be on your guard!... Life does not consist in an abundance of possessions"** (Luke 12:15). About debt, he warns us**, "Owe no one anything, except to love each other" (Rom 13:8).** Jesus tells us clearly to move away from these things and come closer to Him if we seek true freedom. He will bring light into your dark cell. You simply have to invite Him in.

The moment you open that door to your heart and accept Christ, when you take a step of faith and hand your life over to Him, the power of the Holy Spirit will immediately be released and you will be strengthened. If you hand over your worries knowing that God will take care of them, He will. If you leave your pain at His feet, knowing He will take it away, He will. If you cry out to Him asking Him to comfort you, knowing He will wrap His arms around you, then He will. The knowing part is faith.

When the Israelites, led by Joshua toward the Promise Land, arrived at the banks of the Jordan River, the Ark of the Covenant (a chest that held the tablets of stone on which the Ten Commandments were written) was carried ahead of the people by priests, and was their signal to continue forward. God told Joshua to cross the Jordan, so he proceeded in complete faith. He told the priests to fear not the raging waters and to step in, for God was with them. The moment the priests stepped into the water, the Jordan stood still. The water that normally flowed down was piled in a heap so the people could cross on dry ground. The priests did not wait for the water to calm. They stepped in knowing it would. It is *that* faith that frees us.

Move forward, my friend. Leave it all at His feet. What we carry through this life on earth can be a very heavy load to bear without a Savior. Invite Him to accompany you on your journey and watch how paths clear, waters still, and mountains move. Watch how quickly wounds heal and lives change. Watch how darkness becomes light and you become love. Just watch.

"I am the way and the truth and the life."

Jesus

EPILOGUE

A lthough this book is about my personal spiritual journey and my faith in a living God, it may leave some wondering how Robbie is today. It has been seven years since his injury and God's presence has been consistent.

Robbie received academic instruction for the three months he was at Magee, and continued his education for two more months at home thanks to his home instructors, Don Chew and Shelly Vogelei. He returned to his high school that December and graduated on time in 2008. He was accepted at Temple University where his father, grandfather, and great grandfather all attended. Although he began with an interest in architecture, it was quickly discovered that his passion was film. (Robbie had begun quoting movies as soon as he was able to talk at age two.) He excelled in the major and graduated from Temple in 2013 with a GPA of 3.6.

Robbie's college experience had moments of its own that proved we were shaded by God's umbrella. My husband Rob never returned to work as a school teacher and became Robbie's roommate as he needed someone to get him out of bed, shower, shave, dress, and set him up with his laptop in class. He then needed Rob to put him in bed at night and turn him every couple of hours to avoid pressure sores. Rob slept on an air mattress on the dorm room floor for five years, earning himself National

Father of the Year recognition in 2011. Robbie attended classes on his own. He declined an offer for a scribe and took his own notes on his laptop or iPhone, typing with his knuckles. He did get very sick a few times, but God provided. There were calls to doctors, appointments at Magee, and even a couple ambulance rides. He became so sick with an infection one week that he came home to our local hospital. The doctor told him they would have to admit him to administer IV antibiotics for a few days. Robbie asked the doctor to put a pick line in his arm, pack up the medications, and ship them to Temple because he had classes to attend. Rob administered the medication between classes and he made it through another semester with flying colors. It is also amazing that my husband never got sick enough to be unable to be with Robbie and accompanied him through eight semesters. They would pack up the car with all the equipment needed to care for Robbie on Monday mornings, and return home Thursday evenings for the weekend. Meanwhile, I worked two jobs to pick up the slack and I took over the nightshift from Thursday to Monday so Rob could rest. It was five years of this schedule that earned Robbie his college education. What a gift from father to son! Robbie likes to joke that the difficulty of being paralyzed from the chest down is secondary to living with one's father in a dorm room for five years. It was not easy for either of them, but they forged on and succeeded. It was a relationship like no other.

His senior project, a short film called *Sweepstakes*, written by Mark Tumas and produced by Robbie, was elected into the Temple

University Diamond Film festival. It won "best cinematography," "best undergraduate film," and "best film." As I watched Robbie receiving the awards with his team, I believed I was getting a glimpse of his future. He is creative and brilliant and although this is his mother speaking, I truly believe wherever he lands, he will do great things. If he were not completely dependent on Rob and myself as his only caretakers due to the fact that we are unable to afford to pay someone, he would most likely have already gone to New York City or California to chase his dream of making movies. But for now, he is doing everything he can to feed his passion. He watches movies. He studies them. He breaks some of them down scene by scene as a learning experience. He takes screen caps and documents what he has watched. He has written almost a complete script that he intends to produce. He continues to seek employment opportunities as he consistently focuses on what he *can* do. That is why I believe Robbie *will* find himself on a movie set someday.

Robbie has an amazing circle of friends who never forget to invite him to events and gatherings. His friends carry him up and down stairs, drive him to the city, feed him at parties, adjust his feet, put up his hood, take off his jacket, and always pound fists or hug when they part. They look out for him in the most beautiful ways and they have been doing so since they were sixteen years old. Family, passion, dreams, friendships—Robbie embraces them all. He never complains and I watch him carry more people than have ever carried him. My son cannot move, but oh, how he moves me!